THE PROPERTY MANAGEMENT TOOLBOX

A HOW-TO GUIDE FOR ONTARIO
REAL ESTATE INVESTORS AND LANDLORDS

QUENTIN D'SOUZA

THE PROPERTY MANAGEMENT TOOLBOX

A How-To Guide for
Ontario Real Estate Investors and Landlords

The Property Management Toolbox
A How-To Guide for Ontario Real Estate Investors and Landlords

Feedback and Comments: info@theontariolandlordtoolbox.com

THE PROPERTY MANAGEMENT TOOLBOX

A How-To Guide for
Ontario Real Estate Investors and Landlords

By Quentin D'Souza
DREIC Publishing 2014

PREFACE

The original reason for the creation of this book sounds a bit more morbid than I think most book origins do. It was created to act as a manual for my spouse in the event of my death.

It started when I was speaking with a potential joint venture partner about all of the possibilities and potential pitfalls associated with a joint venture deal. My partner asked me, "What would happen to the property if you were to die?" That may sound like a morbid question, but in a joint venture real estate deal, it's a legitimate—and prudent— question. This got me thinking more about the eventuality of my own death, and the possible impact it would have on the business (not to mention my family). I'd been developing systems for several years already, but at that point I hadn't started putting all the information together into a manual.

The next impetus to build this manual came from my wife as I was preparing for a business trip approximately one year after the joint venture partner asked me the question about death. Laura, my wife, and I were preparing for my departure, and we soon realized that much of the preparation was centered on our real estate business. There was so much knowledge I needed to transfer to her, just so I could take a short trip!

It became obvious that since I handle most of the day-to-day affairs of our real estate business, I knew much about our operation that Laura didn't know. Laura was somewhat concerned as I left on that short trip and actually said to me, "What would I do if you passed away? I think I would have to sell all the properties."

Based on what we'd been building for several years, I knew selling wouldn't be the best option for her if I were to pass away, so I wanted to offer her a way to handle the business if I experienced an untimely death.

At that time, I began systematically compiling information for this manual using the best practices I've learned on my own as well as the wealth of knowledge I've gained from other real estate investors in the *Durham Real Estate Investors Club* (DurhamREI. ca), and from personal contacts in the real estate investment industry.

Soon after starting my serious effort towards the manual, I realized that it would be a valuable tool for more than just my eventual demise. It became apparent that when the day comes where I would like a property manager to take over my day-to-day operations, this manual would be invaluable.

With my wife and a future property manager in mind to potentially take over the day to day dealings of our real estate business, the manual has been designed as a system that can be scaled up. What I've found over the years is that with the right systems in place, it's less time consuming to manage several properties than it is to purchase and renovate one property.

We typically renovate every property we buy, and I've found that the process of finding and renovating a property, and putting the first tenant in a property, is more work than managing the rest of the portfolio.

This is somewhat counter to most landlords' experience. As you spend time in real estate investing clubs and speak with other investors, you will find that day-to-day management is usually the biggest headache landlords have. I started to think that my landlording knowledge and my streamlined processes might be unique. This belief was soon borne out by evidence.

When I began to show other landlords the manual I'd created, they were eager to get a copy of it. I was even offered $1,000 at a coffee shop for my original operations manual binder. That was when I knew I had something special. I've shared many of the principles, as well as the idea behind the manual, with hundreds of investors over the years, and experience has proven that this manual makes a great tool for both the average and experienced landlord in Ontario.

True to its origins, this book is a step-by-step manual that lays out the day-to-day operations for small-scale landlords (owning between one and twenty properties) and helps create a solid residential real estate business in Ontario. Over time, though, the scope of the manual has been slightly expanded, and I have added some anecdotes, examples, and more explanation that I think is valuable in teaching the material. Hence, the manual became a book.

ACKNOWLEDGEMENTS

When I started writing this book, I was working full-time, running a real estate investment club, and building a portfolio of properties. Most people were amazed at what I was able to accomplish. There are so many people that I leaned on at different times who have helped and supported me, and I want to thank them for their advice and support.

Starting off, I'd like to thank my incredible wife, Laura, for putting up with all of my ideas. Without her support, I would not have been able to attempt this book. And big hugs and thanks to my boys, Darcy and Lucas.

This book was built on the knowledge of so many real estate investors, landlords, paralegals, lawyers, real estate agents, and property managers that I have met over the years. I know that these people also garnered their knowledge from other people before them, and so on. I have used many people's ideas picked up during phone calls, read online, gathered at meetings, learned about in courses, and even gleaned through conversations at presentations that I was giving. It would be impossible for me to give credit to all of you individually, but I do want to thank you.

I'd be remiss if I didn't thank Don Campbell for starting me down the right path when I began real estate investing. Through his inspiration and organization, I was able to begin my education and meet so many other great people who were also investing in real estate. It provided me a great start and a good beginning support network.

There are so many contributions from people, both big and small, that appear throughout the book. Thank you to the thousands of real estate investors, landlords, and real estate business owners that I have met at the Durham Real Estate Investment Club (DurhamREI.ca). In particular, there are a few people whose education and direction has helped me tremendously: Zander Robertson, Jeff Woods, Andrew Brennan, Kevin Boughen, Trudi Johnston, Val Novak, Aaron Moore, Joey Ragona, Chris Davis, Tahani Aburaneh, Mark Weisleder, Jeff Varcoe, Russell Westcott, Patrick Francey, Michael Dominguez, Tania Hobbs, Mark Loeffler, Ian Szabo, and Gary McGowan.

I wanted to give a very special thank you to Harry Fine of Landlord Solutions. He shared some great notice template resources, when he came to speak at a *Durham Real Estate Investors Club* event. I used his templates as a basis for a number of my own notice templates.

Thanks to a few people who provided me with inspiration and encouragement through their writings and videos: Julie Broad, Dave Peniuk, Tom Karadza, and Nick Karadza. You are a blessing to all Real Estate Investors in Canada, because of who you are and what you are willing to share.

TABLE OF CONTENTS

"The only real security that a man will have
in this world is a reserve of knowledge,
experience, and ability."

— Henry Ford

HOW TO USE THIS BOOK

Goals

While this book is designed to be comprehensive enough to get your real estate business going, it's important to remember to continue your education and keep learning after reading it.

As laws, the market, and other conditions change, landlords must stay up to date. Your understanding will deepen with experience, too. It's vital to continue to furnish that understanding with new and improved knowledge.

With that caveat aside, let's turn our attention to what this book can do for you as a landlord:

1. **Start Up** – By following the teachings of this book, a brand new landlord should be able to confidently start down the path. When you first start as a landlord, there's an overwhelming amount of information to be absorbed, and specific situations must be dealt with in specific ways. Furthermore, these specific instances must be handled differently depending upon the jurisdiction. The suggestions of this book are Ontario-specific.

2. **Expand** – Landlords stop buying properties after purchasing one or two because of the time commitments and headaches typically associated with landlording. By following the

systems, processes, and procedures outlined in this book, small landlords can scale up their operation and manage a portfolio of up to 20 properties with streamlined effort.

By using the right systems and procedures, the day-to-day property management isn't the most difficult aspect of real estate investing. It's more time consuming to find good deals, purchase, and renovate them than to manage the property. This is the opposite of most landlords' experience.

3. **Fix Specific Problems** – Most real estate education focuses on acquiring properties—with a little bit of attention focused on getting a tenant into the property. There are few resources available to assist landlords in understanding and remediating problems specific to landlording.

The landlord may learn what's legal by reading the Residential Tenancy Act, but the law books won't teach efficient procedures for helping the landlord solve problems.

This book is one— if not *the* only—resource available for solving landlord- specific problems.

To sum up: The purpose of this book is that it is to be used as a manual for landlords, or even as a reference for someone about to start a property management company. Yes, the landlording procedures in this book are robust enough for a professional property manager to use as a guide of best practices.

My goal is to furnish you with the right knowledge and understanding so that you can confidently manage a portfolio of properties, whether yours or others. The way to that goal is through thorough explanations of who, what, where, when, why, and how to carry out specific activities. I will provide checklists, sample materials, and anecdotes where helpful to teach the craft of successful landlording.

Parts of This Book

This book is split into three parts:

1. The Art of Landlording

2. Increasing Cash Flow

3. Policies and Procedures

This book is intended to provide you with the correct information. Many landlords simply have the wrong information, and while this book won't eliminate all false information, it will go a long way towards replacing incorrect, impractical, or useless information.

The first section breaks somewhat with the major theme of information transfer. The purpose of this first section is to furnish *understanding*. Most non-fiction books offer strong information —although precious few do so on the topic of landlording— but few provide the correct information along with the lubrication of understanding.

Think of the information as the engine of a car. Yes, it's impressive, but without oil, the engine stops working immediately. Blindly implementing policies and procedures (the information) without understanding the bigger picture or purpose will turn you into an engine without oil.

The first section – The Art of Landlording – is designed to provide you with the oil to lubricate your landlording engine. Note: This section is purposely meant to be brief. I want you to understand the process, but I don't want you to get too philosophical about landlording. This is a business. My advice throughout is to get your work done so you can spend the better part of your time on the important things – family and friends.

The second section – Increasing Cash Flow – provides a mix of understanding and information. The most technically perfect landlord isn't worth the paper a lease is printed on if he or she doesn't maximize cash flow at every opportunity.

The second section provides pure information in the form of strategies for increasing cash flow as well, as an understanding of the *cash flow mentality*. Armed with both understanding and information, you should be able to effectively improve your cash flow bit-by-bit, year-by-year, for an overall better landlording experience.

The third section, Policies and Procedures are tools to make your landlording life easier, but nothing has the power to improve your landlording experience like *more cash*. My personal goal is to improve cash flow on every property every year. These cash flow improvements may be small, but the *cumulative effect* these small improvements lead to huge improvements in a landlord's bottom line and quality of landlording experience.

By far, the largest part of the book is the third part – Policies and Procedures. This section has been designed and laid out as a manual. Each of the specific issues dealt with in that section is set out in an easy-to-understand numbered list. In some instances, the reason behind each directive on the numbered list will be apparent. I've attempted to provide explanations wherever it might enhance the reader's understanding of the purpose of the policy or procedure and why it's effective.

Each policy and procedure is designed to a) improve a landlord's ability to better manage their time, b) improve cash flow, and c) adhere strictly to the Landlord Tenancy Act.

This third section is the bulk of the book, and while you may choose to read through each and every policy at once, it's meant to be used as a reference book. As you go along on your landlording journey, you will encounter problems that you won't know how to begin solving. These are the moments to pull out this manual and begin your study. In some circumstances, the policies you find in this manual will be enough to direct you to solve the problem. In other cases, what you find in this manual will be a starting point for you to deepen your research and understanding.

SECTION 1: OVERVIEW

"Move out of your comfort zone. You can only grow if you are willing to feel awkward and uncomfortable when you try something new."

— Brian Tracy

ART AND SCIENCE

While you'll learn all about the scientific side of landlording later in this book, I want to make you aware of the artistic side of landlording here. Both sides require a consistent dedicated approach that you will be able to improve upon significantly over time.

While science is rule-bound and teachable, art can only be hinted at. An art teacher can point the student toward certain techniques, but the artist must develop his or her own style to become a master. This might sound esoteric, but it's actually quite simple.

In this section, we will focus on the Art and Science of Landlording and work on some skills that you should develop.

"If you are going to be a champion,
you must be willing to pay a greater price."

— Bud Wilkinson

Chapter 1

THE ART AND SCIENCE OF LANDLORDING

Relationships and Systems

There are two categories of activity that a landlord must master to be successful. The first—and most important—is relationships. The second—which acts as a support system to the first—is systems.

Relationships are art. Systems are science.

I can point you toward the basic techniques of correct relationships, but you'll have to develop your own style to master them. Are you naturally boisterous, giving big slaps on the back to people you've just met? I suggest a continued but tempered use of that boisterousness in your relationships. Are you a quiet introvert who excels at listening? Try tailoring your relationship approach to take advantage of this natural inclination.

There are some basic relationship principles that you must apply, however, regardless of your natural inclination:

1. Solution Orientation – It might feel like your ego is being battered and bruised when involved in a dispute, but nothing will tank your efforts faster than having to win a battle of egos.

   Situations arise; your job is to reach the solution whatever situation you encounter. Your job isn't to 'win' the argument. There's an old maxim that states, "You can be right or you can be happy." Getting the solution is what will lead to landlording happiness. Being right and not reaching the solution will do nothing for you in the long run.

2. Civility – Everyone you deal with, including tenants, deserves your respect. Each person has unique life experiences and circumstances. It's not your job to mistreat anyone—ever. This, along with being solution oriented, forms a large part of what we call "professionalism".

3. Staunchness – It's often falsely believed that civility and 'niceness' go hand in hand. Niceness is often associated with giving people a break. The thing to remember is that one can be civil, yet remain staunch.

   To be successful landlord, you don't break the rules you've laid out for the relationship. The lease has stipulations, and your job is to set the boundaries and expectations with the tenant. A lack of staunchness will undermine your efforts at reaching solutions and remaining civil.

The style you use to apply these principles is up to you. Keep these in mind while you develop your art, but application will depend on your level of comfort and your natural inclination.

Relationships are the art of landlording. Systems are the science. In this book, the systems are laid out as policies and procedures. For most imaginable situations (I don't say 'every' because it's inevitable that you'll experience *something* not covered in this book), I've provided a policy or procedure to deal with it.

I'm not asking you to blindly follow the systems provided in this book, though. Wherever necessary, I've provided an explanation in order to furnish you with the *why* as well as the *what, where, when, and how*. It's my belief that understanding the *why* makes you a better landlord.

Let's talk a little bit more about relationships and systems before we delve into the meat of this book.

Relationships 101

I'm a big systems guy. I believe systems and the correct policies to implement them are vital to landlording success; however, I would *not* say systems are the most important aspect of landlording. Why is this my outlook when I'm such a big policy and systems guy ,as you'll see in the last ¾ of the book?

The best systems in the world won't save a landlord if relationships are lacking. This is a relationships business first.

This isn't unique to landlording, either. Every business is a relationship business before a systems business. It's pretty easy to prove this, too. Consider a couple of companies.

Apple – As much as Apple is famous for its flashy products and glamorous product launches, it's the customer experience at the Apple store that sets this business apart. No doubt there have been some bad Apple store experiences over time, but on the whole, most Apple customers will tell you that a trip to the Apple store leaves you feeling like you actually have a relationship with the company and that they'll do what it takes to satisfy and please their clients.

Westjet – Things have changed in Westjet land. These days, Westjet isn't seen in a much—if any—different light than Air Canada, but this wasn't always the situation. Don't believe me? Ask any Westjet customers from Alberta, British Columbia, or Saskatchewan with experiences from Westjet's first decade in business.

Westjet was known for facilitating customers at every point of contact. Customer service people were helpful and friendly. Check-in counter staff was outstanding, and flight attendants were almost celebrities. Moreover, Westjet opened up dozens of new markets and was known for being significantly less expensive than Air Canada. The regional flight landscape of Canada has been dramatically changed by the relationships Westjet created with their clientele.

Were their back-end systems any better than Air Canada's? Did Westjet have superior policies? No – relationship management is what set Westjet apart. Now that Westjet's relationship management has slumped to Air Canada levels, the two competitors both occupy similar positions in Canadian flyers' minds.

These are only two relatively well-known examples. Every business's biggest advantage is its relationship advantage. Real estate investment and landlording are no different.

Cultivating Successful Relationships

It's worth asking: What relationships are vital to a real estate investor's success? Are some relationships more important than others? The answer is that there are several important relationships to consider as a real estate investor and a landlord. Let's take a look at some of them:

1. **Bankers and Mortgage Brokers** – To be successful as a real estate investor, you'll need access to money. To get access to money, it'll be necessary to cultivate strong relationships with those who hold the keys to the bank's purse strings. No, there's no getting around the bank's regulations, but solid relationships can be the difference between smooth financing and clunky, slow financing.

2. **Contractors** – Yes, you'll unquestionably need them. Unless you're an expert on every physical aspect of a property, contractors will be vital to your landlording experience. You must immerse yourself in the business of contractor relations in order to ease the worry of finding and retaining excellent contractors.

   If you build solid relationships with your contractors, they will prioritize your job. Simply put, contractor relationships get things done.

3. **Lawyers and Paralegals** – Who takes care of you when any legal issue comes up? Your lawyer or paralegal, of course. These professionals aren't often considered until a sticky situation comes up. Don't wait until an emergency occurs to cultivate an excellent relationship with legal professionals. Doing so increases the probability that you'll end up with a dud, or worse yet, with a cold and uncaring professional. Excellent and timely legal advice can be like a defibrillator to a heart attack victim – it can save your life. But just like a defibrillator, legal advice isn't worth much if it's not available at the right moment.

4. **Realtors** – A great realtor will make buying and selling property so much easier. To be clear – it's not difficult to find a realtor, but it might be a little tricky to find an *excellent*

realtor. This isn't because there aren't plenty of excellent realtors; it's because there are far more generalist realtors than investment specialists. You need to find the right investment specialist realtor and cultivate a relationship. Remember – relationships go two ways. A busy, successful full time investment specialist realtor will require you to bring as much to the table as he or she does. Be active in holding up your end of the deal, and you'll become a realtor relationship master.

5. **Tenants** – While each of the relationships above is important, and while they are all essential to effective landlording, not one of them is more important than your relationship with your tenant.

   As a landlord in the trenches for the past decade, I've heard all kinds of stories about landlords, both successes and failures. The common thread in each of the landlording success stories is excellent tenant relationships.

   As with Apple and Westjet, it's your clients that matter most. Yes, your tenants *are* your clients. They should not be looked down upon or be objects of derision. They're not to be taken advantage of or mistreated. Tenants are to be respected and treated like the golden ticket that they are.

   Remember the great children's book and movie *Charlie and the Chocolate Factory?* In the story, a young boy named Charlie receives a golden ticket from the famous candy maker, Willie Wonka. The golden ticket allows Charlie to tour the chocolate factory with four other children. Through good behavior and perseverance, Charlie eventually wins the grand prize and is allowed to move to the chocolate factory with his 4 grandparents and parents. Charlie and his family won big, but they never would have won if Charlie hadn't taken care of his golden ticket.

Your tenants are *your* golden ticket. Take care of them, maintain and develop excellent relationships with them, and stick with them. By developing the right relationships and implementing the right policies and systems, you'll find that they're not as bad as most landlords claim. Quite the opposite – most tenants are outstanding. Just learn the art of picking the right tenants and watch them prove themselves.

Does this mean you'll never run into a bad tenant? Of course not. You can't completely avoid negative outcomes in any business, but on the whole, tenants do as they're supposed to—take care of the property and pay the rent. This leaves you to do your job – maintain the property and build a strong relationship.

Landlording is a systems- and policies-dependent business, but it's far more a relationships-dependent business. Remain faithful to this fact and spend significant energy building and maintaining relationships, and you'll find yourself successful. Use policies and systems as effective tools. Don't put the tools ahead of the relationships.

The Great Landlording Myth

Given the above discussion about relationships in landlording, it's important to consider the most common myth landlords believe in and how it might affect your business. It's an extension of the relationship issue.

What's the most common myth? It's the dreaded tenant vandalism. Here's the thing with tenant vandalism: When it happens, it's often bad enough to set the landlord back in a big way.

What is normal is ordinary wear and tear. It might not seem like much to the tenant, but to you as the landlord, it seems like you're constantly updating and renovating. This is as it should be. It's a landlord's job to keep the property in good shape. Regular wear and tear is inevitable, but it can be greatly minimized by correct landlording practices. This manual will deal with these correct practices in detail. I will also endeavor to make clear which damage expenses are the tenant's responsibility and which are the landlord's responsibility.

Regular wear and tear, or even unintentional damage isn't so bad. Your goal as a proactive and cash flow conscious landlord is to be able to continually improve and maintain the property without spending any money beyond what the property produces.

Willful vandalism is another story. This is when a tenant is angry with the landlord and decides to take revenge on the landlord. It's a terrible situation for the landlord because even if insurance covers it (make sure it does), you'll still spend significant effort remediating the problem. It's never a good thing.

Keep one thing in mind – as a victim, you have the right to prosecute for any instance of vandalism. It's not as though you don't know who the perpetrators are, and it's not like you wouldn't have a rock-solid case against them, especially if you record everything (as will be discussed in detail). This is what's known as 'the stick', one half of 'the carrot and the stick'. The great legal stick is long, and it strikes hard. Regardless of how angry a tenant is, few are dumb or crazy enough to intentionally bring the stick down on themselves.

A proactive landlord can take precautions against letting the dumb and crazy into the property. If you do happen to be so unlucky that one gets past your radar, you can take preemptive measures to protect yourself, such as being diligent on insurance, keeping all records, and following correct process, all things that this book will discuss.

The bottom line on this myth of tenant vandalism is that it's rare, and if it does happen, you can survive it with correct preparation. It's not the bogeyman many landlords make it out to be.

Belief in this myth is most common among prospective landlords, but many *existing* landlords believe it, too. Of those that do, the largest group is the landlords with one to three properties. It's as though they think they've 'just been lucky' up till now, and they fear they'll end up stuck with a tenant vandal. This fear is enough to stop many landlords from acquiring more properties. Remember, one of the objectives of this book is to help you acquire more property if that's one of your goals.

If you're scared of tenant vandals, it's time to move beyond the fear. Read the entire book and learn how to put *yourself* in the driver's seat rather than letting a fear of the highly unlikely drive *you*.

The Non-Myth of Landlording

The frequency of rental property vandalism is the biggest myth that landlords believe, but there's a 'non-myth' that not enough tenants are aware of when they should be. This non-myth is non-payment of rent.

This is the most common problem you'll face as a landlord. Of course you're aware of it, but perhaps you're not cognizant enough of the pervasiveness of this problem. Here's the cold hard fact: Over 75% of the cases that find their way to the Landlord Tenant Board tribunal process are related to non-payment of rent.

No pay = big problem for landlords. Your business is 100% dependent upon the consistent and timely payment of monthly rent by your tenants. Yes, you take precautions and have a reserve fund so you won't go out of business if a tenant or two is late on rent, but you can't afford too many months with missed or late rent payments.

I've dedicated a significant portion of this book to dealing with the common problem of non-payment of rent. You will read about the finer details of how to deal with non-payment of rent later in this book, but it's worth pointing out the main aspects here:

1. Speed – It's vital that you act immediately when a tenant fails to pay rent. In fact, the system is set up such that you *will lose* if you fail to act quickly. However, if you do act swiftly, there's a chance that you might not lose any money at all.

2. Process – Failing to follow process can slow down the eviction process. Even one missing element means starting the whole process over again, pushing back the timelines. Remember, speed is the most critical element when dealing with non-payment of rent.

3. Records – Failing to keep excellent records of the non-payment problem as it evolves could lead to a failure of process, which leads to a failure of speed.

Remember that as a landlord in Ontario, you have the right to collect the last month's rent when tenancy begins. This means that even if a tenant doesn't pay rent for one month and leaves within that month, you won't be without payment. However, if you dawdle on the process and don't get the tenant out (and a new one in), you'll be stuck with a) a tenant in the property and b) no income.

It's true that you have legal recourse to claim that missed rent, but oftentimes the cost and time commitment associated with chasing a month's worth of rent isn't enough to make it worthwhile.

Acting quickly, following process, and keeping records are the key elements to ensuring that the relatively common problem of non-payment of rent doesn't cripple your business. At no time is it more important to follow an excellent system than when dealing with the problem of non-payment of rent. Systems are always essential, but when it comes to a recurring issue, systems become crucial.

I just mentioned the importance of systems, but don't forget our earlier discussion about relationships, which still far and away trumps systems in terms of importance. The right relationships will minimize the non-payment of rent issue and help to resolve the problem when does occur.

Recognizing the several types of non-paying tenants will also help you take care of this issue:

1. Bad Habit Tenants – Some tenants are just late. They've never missed rent, and they never will miss rent, but somewhere along the way they've developed the bad habit of paying late.

   Does this mean you just accept their late payments and continue on with business? No, these tenants need re-education, and there are tools available to help you do this. You also have the recourse to evict those tenants if you find they can't be re-educated.

Both eviction and re-education will require you to properly follow the process.

2. Partial Payment Tenants – Some tenants are in real financial difficulty and want to pay rent, but simply can't. It's a sad fact of landlording that you'll run into people with significant financial problems. Of course, you want to screen for tenants that have the ability to pay consistently, but even they may experience financial difficulty through job loss or some other problem.

   Receiving something is better than receiving nothing, but it remains essential that you act quickly and follow process to ensure you don't lose income.

3. Bad Tenants – These people enter into a contract knowing they'll never pay their rent. They will lie or use any other means necessary to stay in the property without paying rent.

   Bad tenants are often charismatic. They've caused problems for landlords before, and they know exactly what emotional triggers will cause an inexperienced landlord to let them off the hook.

   I made the common rookie landlord mistake of accepting the word of a bad tenant at face value. As a result, I didn't correctly follow the process and ended up being without rent payment for 4 months.

The important thing to remember is that you begin the process the day after rent is due, regardless of which type of non-payer you're dealing with.

You might say, "But Quentin, you said this business was about relationships. Won't I be ruining a relationship if I start the process immediately?"

No. Relationships go two ways and are founded on trust. It's your job to maintain the property and provide good, solid housing for your tenants. It's their job to pay their rent and take care of the property. They've signed a lease agreement stating they'll pay rent, so if they don't you have every right and reason to remedy the situation.

Giving tenants a break doesn't improve the relationship, it makes it worse – every time. If a tenant doesn't pay rent on the 1st of the month, you start implementing the n$/eviction process on the 2nd. This is the only way to deal with this problem, regardless of the tenant and what they might say to convince you that they'll pay soon.

How Landlords Waste Time

One of the overarching themes of this book is time. To be an effectual landlord, you must be a master of your own time and use time productively. If you unsystematically react to situations rather than apply time-management and efficiency principles, you'll find the business completely overwhelming. On the other hand, if you apply the correct principles of time management and efficiency, you'll find you can get more done than you ever thought possible.

The most egregious mistake is inefficiency in handling rent collection. Remember, it's the tenant's job to get the rent payment to you. It's not your job to track down the rent payment from the tenant. You have an obligation to provide clear instructions as to how tenants can pay their rent, but as long as you're clear, it's not your job to go pick up the rent.

One of the main goals of this book is to introduce you to the principles of management that will allow you to scale up your business. This is a good metric to judge your actions by: Ask yourself, "Can I scale this action up to 10, 15, or 20 properties?" Let's use the example of picking up rent cheques. It might not be that big of a deal to pick up one or two rent payments every month, but when you scale that up, it quickly becomes unmanageable.

Improper use of time is probably the biggest self-inflicted problem that landlords experience. The most colossal time waste is chasing rent payments around. Given our discussion of late rent payments above, it's easy to see why landlords make the mistake of rushing out to pick up rent cheques; they're worried. Just remember, if you start picking up the rent, you'll be training the tenant in exactly the behavior you don't want. If you immediately start the N4/eviction process when rent doesn't arrive, you'll be training the tenant for exactly the behavior you *do* want.

Relationships and Systems Provide Time and Money

Time and money are the two resources you must learn to maximize as a landlord. Relationships and systems—in that order—are the way to augment time and money. This book is designed to help you improve relationships and systems in order to maximize time and money.

Without further introduction or overview, let's start our discussion of cash flow.

SECTION 2:
INCREASING CASH FLOW

"Cash is King."

— BUSINESS MAXIM

LANDLORDING IS INVESTING

You may be tempted to think that because you are renting out a property, you are simply a landlord. The truth is that you wouldn't have bought the property if you had not been planning to make money on it. Let's be real here, you aren't going through all the trouble of learning these strategies and processes just to provide a great rental property for someone else. Your hope is that by good property management, you will be able to keep expenses down and increase your cash flow so that your little rental property business produces income for you every month. You are anticipating that many years of mortgage pay down and property appreciation will give you a really good investment.

Try to remember that each property that you own is a little business. You have invested money into that business with the purpose of *making* money. Treat your business with care and examine every expense to find efficiencies. Strive to maximize the income that you will receive from your tenants.

"Opportunity is missed by most people."

— Thomas Edison

Chapter 2

HOW AND WHY TO INCREASE CASH FLOW

Increase Cash Flow

Those of us heavily involved in real estate investing tend to take the notion of cash flow for granted. As it turns out, though, many early investors fail to pay enough attention to this aspect of real estate investment.

There's so much misinformation out there about real estate investing. It seems a lot of new investors think of real estate as a get-rich-quick scheme. They believe the only thing to do to become rich is to simply purchase a piece real estate. It doesn't work that way. Without a serious and committed strategy for maximizing cash flow, the real estate investing experience will inevitably be difficult and troublesome.

The trouble arises due to a misunderstanding of what constitutes true cash flow. In order to achieve real cash flow, real estate investors *must* factor in not only the monthly expenses, but also contingencies. Depending on the region in which one invests, this contingency amount can be in the neighborhood of 10% or more of total revenue for the property. The contingency number is derived from the percentage chance of vacancy, as well as, a percentage of total revenue dedicated to unforeseen maintenance.

A savvy real estate investor sees the unforeseen.

Weak cash flow can end a real estate investing career. A slight downturn in the market, coupled with weak cash flow can turn an investment portfolio into negative cash flow very quickly. Negative cash flow properties are known as 'alligators' because they eat real estate investors. Taking money every month from your own job's pay cheque to pay for an 'investment' is usually enough to force an investor to throw in the towel.

But let's think about cash flow from the positive side, too. By having a sharp focus on improving cash flow, an investor can drastically improve his or her prospects of having a successful investment experience. With small changes over an entire portfolio, the cumulative effect of cash flow improvement makes a big difference long term.

Let's take a look at two scenarios, one positive and one negative.

Scenario 1: Investor Has Weak Cash Flow

Let's imagine an investor named Joe who owns five properties. Joe, like so many other investors, got involved in real estate investing because he heard it was a great way to make a lot of money. He heard that you buy a property, rent it out, and over time the property appreciates. At the same time, the mortgage is getting paid down which results in the owner getting rich.

Joe was partially right. Investors can make a lot of money in real estate, but the actual story is much more complex than Joe realized.

As a result of Joe's weak understanding of real estate investments, he ended up purchasing properties with weak cash flow. This happens to investors for many reasons. For Joe, it happened because he didn't understand what kind of property produces strong cash flow.

Joe bought properties in overvalued areas where the rent/purchase price ratio was too low. In addition, he was in a hurry to buy, so he took out mortgages with unfavorable interest rates. As a result, his cash flow across 5 properties was only $250, or $50 per property.

When he started buying properties, Joe didn't expect to have to pay for things like vacancies or maintenance. As a result, his estimated cash flow was much lower than his real cash flow. He was cash flow negative when you do a real calculation of cash flow, which includes a percentage for vacancy allowance and maintenance expenses.

Joe squeaked by for a time.

Unfortunately, two years into Joe's real estate investing career, there was a significant financial downturn. This downturn was surprising to no one, since the economy is constantly cycling up and down, but here were a couple of consequences that Joe didn't expect as a result of the financial down:

a. He was forced to drop his rents on average $100 per property in order to keep tenants.

b. He lost his job because the company he worked for became unprofitable in the slower economy.

With the $100 drop in average rents, Joe now had a portfolio that was $250 negative in cash flow. His initial thought was, "Well that's not bad. I can afford to just pay the extra $250 out of my pocket until the market picks up."

When he got fired two weeks later and he looked more closely at his financial picture, he soon realized that he couldn't afford to pay the $250 out of pocket. His personal savings would be completely wiped out within 3 months, and he needed to drastically change his lifestyle.

As a result of his immediate need, Joe quickly and correctly assessed that he needed to sell all of his investment properties. Unfortunately, the properties' values also dropped when the economy turned, so he was forced to sell for less than what he paid. In addition, there were penalties for paying off the mortgages ahead of the original term.

Joe eventually walked away from all five of his investment properties with enough cash to live for an additional six months, which he hoped would be enough to see him through until he got another job and got back on his feet.

Scenario 2: Investor Has Strong Cash Flow

Now let's imagine another investor named Jane, who also owned five investment properties.

Jane had also heard that investment real estate was a great way to make a lot of money, but unlike Joe, she didn't immediately jump into buying investment properties. First, she learned about the power of cash flow, mortgage financing, and what makes a great investment property. Next, she applied those rules to her investments.

Jane made sure she had at least $250 positive cash flow on *each* of her investments to begin with, and she did a new analysis every few months to see if she could bring in new efficiencies to improve her cash flow. Over her entire portfolio, Jane had $1000 of positive cash flow.

When the economic downturn came, Jane also had to drop her rents by $100 dollars per property, and she also lost her job.

The difference was that Jane didn't need to sell her investments because she was still collecting $500 per month of positive cash flow *after* accounting for vacancies and maintenance along with all other expenses.

Jane did struggle after losing her job, but she was able to keep her investment properties. It took her a few months to find another job, but once she was back on her feet, she was able to purchase a few more investment properties since prices were in a good place and her cash flow was strong.

When the market picked up and appreciated—two years after the initial downturn in the economy— Jane became richer by $100,000 and her entire portfolio went up.

What If the Market Goes Up?

I provided examples of two different investors during a difficult time with a weak market: one with poor cash flow and the other with excellent cash flow. I could just as easily have provided the same example in a strong market.

It's commonly known in real estate investing circles that a strong market will cover up a lot of poor practices and investing sins. Even Joe would survive during a strong market with rents and values going up, but Jane would thrive much more so.

A whole world of new opportunities would open up for Jane during a great market. With regular reanalysis of her portfolio, Jane would be able to raise rents, refinance with better mortgages (saving more money), and probably be able to continue buying more great properties.

With increased cash flow, Jane could dedicate more money to property improvements, thereby attracting better tenants over the long term and raising rents again. She could also devote more money to mortgage pay down, which might enable her to save hundreds of thousands over the course of her investing career and purchase even more properties because her debt-to-equity ratios would be so strong.

There are a number of ways Jane could improve her business further by reinvesting her extra cash flow back into the business. This shows that being hyper-focused on strong cash flow is equally as important during the good times as it is during the bad times.

How to Improve Cash Flow

Hopefully from the above discussion and examples, you see *why* it's important to have excellent cash flow. Now let's focus on *how to* improve cash flow.

To increase cash flow, you can either raise revenue or decrease expenditures. These are the only two possible ways to increase cash flow. Too often, we tend to think solely of raising revenues, but a dollar saved is every bit as valuable to the bottom line as a dollar earned. Please keep that in mind as you search for greater efficiencies in your process to increase cash flow. There are some tried and true methods for improving cash flow, and I will discuss them below, but please remember that you may discover other methods that work better for you in your particular situation. As long as it's ethical, fair, and safe, there's no limit to the ways you can improve cash flow.

Here are some of the most commonly effective ways to raise revenues:

- Determine the correct rent and raise rent if possible
- Renovate to the right level for the tenant profile
- Offer furnished suites or rent-to-own
- Provide coin-operated laundry
- Rent out advertising space, cell tower space, parking, basement storage, or garage storage

Here are some of the most commonly effective ways to decrease expenditures:

- Check all invoices and statements and ask yourself, "Is this necessary?"
- Skip a mortgage payment if it's an option
- Re-amortize your mortgage to lower monthly payments on mortgage renewal.

"The road to success is lined with
many tempting parking spaces."

— Unknown

Chapter 3

RAISING REVENUE

Raise Revenue –
Determine Correct Rent and Raise Rent if Possible

Additional Revenue Potential: $25+ per month

It's important to determine the correct rent for each property. If your rent is too high, you might have longer vacancies and therefore a loss of income. Some investors pride themselves on having the absolute highest rents. This is great as long as they're not experiencing longer vacancies or more frequent tenant turnover. It doesn't take much time for a vacant suite to counteract the positive effect of having such a high rent.

Think of it this way: Investor A keeps rents at the absolute top of the market while Investor B keeps rents about $50 lower. Each investor has 5 properties, which means in a 100% occupancy scenario, Investor A earns $3000 more per year than Investor B.

However, Investor A could have a scattering of months of vacancy on at least a couple of properties or more frequent tenant turnover. Assuming the average rent is $1000 per suite, it would only take 3 total months of vacancy to remove the benefit of the $50 per month higher rent. This is in addition to all of the costs associated with finding a new tenant each time.

In other words, it's ultimately more profitable to have slightly lower rents on a property so that it will be rented out immediately, every time it's vacated. This is the balance I always try to strike. By keeping current on my rental market and constantly adjusting rents to just the right amounts, I've found that balance. This is the approach I recommend for all landlords.

Contrarily, if your rent is too low, it's likely you'll have no problem finding a tenant right away, but it's also likely you'll lose money every month.

Here are the top tips for determining correct rent:

- Ask a realtor you're working with to go to the MLS comparables for some recently leased properties in your rental's area.

- Play 'secret shopper' and visit some competing properties to assess how they compare with yours.

- Reassess cash flow considering changes in expenses, etcetera. I survey the immediate area for comparables through rental sites, make calls to nearby properties, and ask my circle of knowledgeable landlords.

- Look at the ads in Kijiji, Craigslist, Rentcheck, Viewit, Rentboard, newspapers, and MLS for places in the same neighborhood with the same basic characteristics (number of bedrooms, washrooms, size). Find the average, and then adjust that number based on the condition of your property. Supply and demand will affect the rent.

- Raise the rent if re-renting and try marketing at the new price for a while. If you're not getting many bites after a couple weeks, then lower the price a bit.

- Ask the neighbours what they pay in rent (my rentals are in neighbourhoods that have a lot of other rentals, so often I ask people what they pay).

- Consider other factors, such as laundry (we provide en suite laundry in our units —it is relatively cheap to provide and tenants will pay extra for the convenience). The same goes for a dishwasher and lots of parking.

Above all, the property must be cash flow positive: it has to cover mortgage, taxes, insurance, *your management fee*, maintenance allowance, vacancy allowance, and any other fees for the property (including utilities paid by tenants in their own name).

Once you've gathered all the information needed, you can make your new rent calculation. From anecdotal evidence, research on competitive websites, and classified ads, as well as advice from your property manager (if you use one), you can then decide upon the correct rental amount. I generally try to ask for slightly more than market ($25-$50 higher) due to the level of finishes in my rental properties.

I recommend you finish your property to a higher level than the average, and then ask slightly more than market rent, as I do. This is the best combination for maximizing revenues while decreasing the unnecessary expenditure of long vacancies.

Raise Revenue – Renovate to the Right Level

Additional Revenue Potential: $25-$100 per month

To maximize cash flow, it's imperative that you act strategically in every respect. Your renovation strategy is one of the most important strategic aspects to consider. Renovating to the right level is both a revenue maximization and expense minimization process. It's important to strike the right balance in your renovations in order to maximize profitability

Renovating is a large topic, and there are other books like *From Renos to Riches: The Canadian Real Estate Investor's Guide to Practical and Profitable Renovations* by Ian Szabo and *Fix & Flip: The Canadian How-To Guide for Buying, Renovating, and Selling Property For Fast Profit* by Mark Loeffler and Ian Szabo that are dedicated to this aspect of real estate investing. For now, let's consider only two broad categories a successful landlord must consider when renovating:

1. Over Renovating – While I'm a big believer in renovating rental properties, it's absolutely imperative that you don't spend too much money on renovations. I'm not suggesting you operate a slum, but as a landlord, you must consider whether your renovations are actually adding to your bottom line. The goal of renovations should be to improve the long-term prospects of profitability. Even on a lower tenant profile, renovations are necessary to maintain a better than average property.

   I've seen people put granite countertops in a low-end rental property. It looks nice, but the cost of it will never be recouped in the rent, and at the end of the day, the tenants may not really even appreciate it. Rental properties often take a beating, and tenants will inadvertently damage the property. In the end, the landlord would have been better to put faux granite laminate in the rental property rather than installing high end finishes in properties that attract a different tenant profile.

2. Under Renovating – If you're trying to attract a higher end tenant, it's important that your renovations reflect this attempt. Landlords in prestigious neighborhoods will tell you that the property must include certain features, or it will be impossible to rent. Without the correct renovations strategy in these types of properties, attracting top tenants and above average rents will be very difficult.

It's possible to over renovate on high-end properties as well. So it's important to carefully analyze your renovation strategy and tenant profile before writing cheques. Of the two just mentioned, over renovating is a far greater problem. Not many investors are (or should be) seeking the high-end market, which puts many investors in the range of starter home tenants.

In this larger segment of the rental market, it's far more likely to over renovate than under renovate. I'm not sure whether it's due to the current television shows on television today, but having your tenants 'oh' and 'ah' when they walk through a property may make for a good reveal on a TV show, but if it doesn't increase your cash flow significantly, it is not the right thing for a rental property.

Raise Revenue – Furnished Suites

Additional Revenue Potential: $400-$1000 per month

If your property is correctly situated and renovated, you may consider the unique strategy of renting it as a furnished suite.

Setting up a furnished suite involves extra expense, a different style of management, and setting up the correct contacts in order to be profitable. However, if it's done correctly, furnished suites can be a highly profitable strategy as rents are often significantly higher than rents for the same property type with an unfurnished suite.

Why?

The furnished suite client is looking for a completely problem-free experience for a shorter time. Typically, you're not renting to an individual tenant so much as a company looking for shorter-term accommodation for one of its employees or consultants.

This strategy works best if your rental properties are situated in an area that will have a high number of visiting consultants or visiting managers from other cities. In Ontario, two good examples are downtown Toronto with its high level of business activity and the KWC (Kitchener-Waterloo-Cambridge) area with its tech sector. Plenty of international trade takes place from this location, and there are therefore more visiting professionals who require a temporary "home away from home" rental accommodation.

Most markets will be able to sustain a certain demand for furnished suites, but places like downtown Toronto and KWC have larger markets than most cities. My own town of Whitby, Ontario has a small market for furnished suites. The most visible company serving this segment of the market in Whitby can be found at www.carolsfurnishedrentals.com.

Raise Revenue – Rent-To-Own

Additional Revenue Potential: $200-$500 per month

As with furnished suites, Rent-To-Own is a strategy that has the potential to drastically improve cash flow, but as with furnished suites, it also requires a specialist approach and favorable conditions to properly pull it off.

There are books dedicated to this strategy. I recommend you read Mark Loeffler's *Investing in Rent to Own Property* for further discussion of the benefits and drawbacks of the strategy. For now, a brief explanation will suffice for our purposes.

Rent-to-own is exactly as it sounds. A tenant rents a property with the intention of eventually owning it. To that end, the landlord collects rental income along with a portion of the rent to be used later as payment against the property.

In most RTO (Rent-to-Own) programs, appreciation is built into the contract. Therefore, the real estate investor is setting a sale price before they officially sell the property.

The end result of a successful RTO is that cash flow is significantly higher than a normal rental property, but it would be remiss of me not to mention that this strategy does have its fair share of pitfalls and detractors.

Unfortunately, it's very common that RTO tenants are ultimately unable to purchase the property they'd been renting to own, which in many circumstances has led to disagreements about how the extra (non-rent) portion of payments should be distributed. The real estate investor specifies in the contract that the purchase portion is non-refundable. But when a contract is broken, the tenant-buyer of the RTO property often disputes the allocation of the purchase portion they've paid. And the result affects relationships and could even lead to a legal battle.

Personally, this strategy isn't my favourite because it's an active strategy and isn't creating long-term wealth, but rather generating active income. I don't like to turn properties over, preferring instead to hold onto them for the long term once I own them.

This is why I put so much emphasis on properly managing rental properties and why I'm writing this landlord's guide. If an investor wants to create long-term wealth in real estate, it's imperative they hold for a long time while managing their portfolio well.

The biggest warning I have for you against the strategy is to always conduct yourself ethically. Never set up a tenant-buyer to fail. If after a careful analysis of the possibility of an applicant closing on the property, you find them unlikely to purchase the property after a set time, please don't go forward with the deal. This amounts to just unethically and wrongly taking people's money.

I find that too high of a percentage of RTO deals end with the tenant-buyer not purchasing the property. I place most of the burden of this problem on the shoulders of the investors operating the RTOs. All too many investors are happy to take a tenant-buyer's money without concern about whether or not they'll ever eventually own the property.

This doesn't mean there's no place for the RTO strategy. RTO is a strategy that can add greatly to your cash flow on an individual property, but it must be treated carefully and with an impeccable level of business ethics. I've personally done a few RTO deals and they've worked well and ended with the tenant eventually buying the property. The main reason I'd recommend trying the RTO strategy is if the property isn't cash flowing properly and the landlord needs to improve the cash flow. The additional portion paid by the tenant-buyer can often be enough to turn a poorly cash flowing property into a stronger cash flowing property.

Raise Revenue – Coin Operated Laundry

Additional Revenue Potential: $50+ per month

For smaller buildings with 1 or 2 suites, I recommend putting the laundry in the suite. This is considered a high-end feature and will allow you to rent the suite at a premium. The additional rent garnered from having laundry in-suite should be considered a suitable replacement for the extra income that a coin-operated laundry would bring.

I recommend *against* coin-operated laundry in a building with one or two suites. These are the reasons:

1. **Cost** – Keep in mind that coin-operated machines aren't just normal machines with a coin-operated device attached. You have to buy the machine as a complete unit with the coin-operated functionality built into it. These machines are often double the cost of a regular washer and dryer. They can be bought used for $1000 a pair, but new ones can cost $1000 or more per machine. In the case of smaller buildings (one or two units), a good landlord's best bet for additional income is to add laundry in-suite because it's unlikely to recoup the cost of the coin-operated machines with profits because of their necessary maintenance.

2. **Maintenance** – There are two aspects of maintenance that landlords must consider before adding coin-operated laundry facilities. 1) Due to their cost, it's far wiser to repair these machines rather than replace them, yet the maintenance and repair people are specialists and therefore charge more. This cost is only worthwhile in a building with minimum three suites. 2) Somebody has to collect the money from the machines. This may seem like a small chore, but the goal of this book and my system is to reduce your time commitment. I want your landlording practices to be highly efficient. Again, the better solution for small buildings is to have laundry in-suite and then charge a premium on rent for it.

So the caveat to coin-operated laundry is that the property must have at least three units. If the building has more than three units, a coin-operated system might be the best possible way to maximize laundry income while minimizing renovations expenses. Rather than adding more rent by having laundry in-suite, you can improve income through coin-operated laundry while not having to spend money renovating the suites for in-suite laundry.

The average family of four will do anywhere between five and fifteen loads of laundry per week. If you charge one dollar per load, this amounts to a minimum of $10 per week (wash and dry) for each family that resides in one of your suites. If you extend the income out over an entire year, it amounts to $520 per year per suite. If you own 15 suites, this amounts to $7,800 per year. Not an insignificant amount of money as long as it doesn't take too much of your time as a landlord to manage the coin-operated systems.

Some tenants might be put off by having to pay for laundry, but as a creative landlord, you can sell the extra cost to tenants in any way that works and provides value to the tenants. For example, you can explain to tenants that you use the extra income for extra property upgrades. Provide specific examples of upgrades you or other landlords have done with laundry income and discuss your future plans for upgrades with the laundry money. You may also explain to tenants that having a coin-operated system prevents abuse and overuse of the machines.

Raise Revenue –
Consider Adding an Accessory Apartment

Additional Revenue Potential: $600-$1500 per month

Many jurisdictions (notably within the Greater Toronto Area) allow basement apartments, often referred to as accessory apartments, on almost all single-family properties now. The need for more affordable housing has been identified by various city and town planning departments, therefore accessory apartments are now highly acceptable and legal as long as they meet the city's requirements.

Adding an accessory apartment is another big topic. For now, it's sufficient to mention that an accessory apartment can be the difference between a property having positive cash flow or not. It can be the difference between a property barely squeaking by on cash flow or being a cash flow star in your portfolio.

The real trick to successfully adding an accessory apartment is getting it funded without having to pay cash out of pocket. There are several ways to do this, and again it's a detailed topic covered in much greater detail later, but for now let's mention two commonly available and proven methods:

1. Mortgage Plus Improvements – This is a mortgage that will fund not only your purchase price, but also the renovations necessary to improve the property. In some cases, the improvements might include adding an accessory apartment.

2. Joint Venture Partner Funding – If you're purchasing the property with a joint venture partner who'll be providing the money, it's often viable to have the partner kick in extra to cover the renovations needed to build an accessory apartment on the property.

Adding an accessory apartment is a tried and true method for increasing cash flow. This additional cash flow effectively raises the value of the property over the long term. There is really no downside to adding an accessory apartment as long as you can do it without breaking your own bank or breaking any zoning or construction laws.

Raise Revenue – Parking Spaces

Additional Revenue Potential: $50+ per month

There are a few scenarios when renting parking spaces that makes this strategy make sense.

1. **Downtown Condo** – As landlord of a condo in the downtown area of any major city (and many minor cities), you should definitely be charging for parking. In Toronto, this isn't even an option; it's a no-questions-asked necessity. Keep in mind that in Toronto, parking isn't considered a normal amenity so you have every right to charge for parking as a landlord. Of course, it's highly preferable to rent to the tenant who's living in the condo unit, but if that's not possible, it's also acceptable to rent to someone else. Just keep in mind your time commitment and how much time it will take to organize the management of the parking space. The exact same rules just discussed can also be applied to a storage facility in a downtown condo.

2. **Downtown House** – I wouldn't charge a tenant extra for parking for a downtown house. I believe it's reasonable to expect a parking spot for renting a house. It is, however, acceptable to rent a *second* parking spot to a tenant if they have another vehicle. Or, if the tenant won't or doesn't want to rent a second, third, or fourth parking spot, the landlord is well within reason to rent that spot to a different person.

Any house near a busy downtown area will be a good spot to rent parking to people working in downtown buildings.

3. **Suburban House** – Even if your rental property isn't in a busy downtown area, it might still be possible to rent parking spaces. In this scenario, though, you will be looking for a different type of parking space rental. Whereas the other types will typically work best for day parkers who will come to the parking spot and leave every week day, a suburban house might be a better fit for someone who needs a long-term parking spot. These spots are usually needed more for trailers, boats, RVs, or trucks.

4. **Townhouse** – Another scenario is a townhouse condo where you own two parking spots. In this case, you may give one parking spot to the tenant and offer to rent the second spot to the same tenant if they have a need for more than one parking spot. If they don't want to rent the spot, you can rent it to someone else.

In all cases, you'll be able to earn somewhere between $50 and $200 per month. The higher the cost of parking in the area, the more you'll be able to charge for your parking spot.

Raise Revenue – Garage Rental

Additional Revenue Potential: $100-$300 per month

Garages are commonly used now as a secondary source of revenue on rental properties. The biggest consideration to keep in mind about renting garages is that the garage be detached. Renting out an attached garage to a tenant not living in the property will likely lead to problems. Your tenants won't feel secure if an attached garage is being rented to another person. This is much less of an issue when renting a detached garage.

The second consideration is that storage rentals don't fall under the landlord-tenant act, which means they're governed by a different set of provincial laws. This doesn't mean you shouldn't rent a garage, but it does mean that you should be aware of the different laws. It can be an added complexity for you as a landlord because you have to learn a whole new set of laws in order to operate your business.

For this reason, I suggest seeking to rent a garage to a tenant first. Failing that, you may seek another renter for the garage. The following is my list of types of garage rental scenarios from most preferable to minimally preferable:

1. **Rent to Tenant** – As previously mentioned, this is the most preferable situation. The tenant may store anything he or she likes in the garage, so long as no laws are broken and there are no complaints from the neighbors. The biggest benefit of renting to the tenant is that you can include the cost of the garage rental in the normal lease. This means you don't have a separate collection for the garage rent, and you don't have to deal with the separate laws that govern storage rentals or follow up with contract changes with tenant turnover.

2. **Storage for Non-Tenant** – The second most preferable scenario is to rent to a non-tenant for the sole purpose of storage. These renters are looking for storage space for work related materials, cars, boats, and household goods—basically anything that needs storage. As long as they don't store dangerous goods or break any laws, you shouldn't have any trouble with these types of garage

renters. In this case, your agreement with the renter will not be covered in normal landlord tenant law, so ensure that you understand the laws governing garage rentals before you rent as storage space.

3. **Workshop for Non-Tenant** – This is the least preferable of the three scenarios in which you might want to rent the garage. This means you're willing to let your renter use the garage to actively do work in your garage. The biggest concern here is that your renter might be operating a business out of the garage, which you most definitely don't want. It might also cause problems if the renter is loud, creates increased traffic or mess around the outside of the building. Given the right circumstance, though, it might work to rent for the purposes of a personal workshop. Please only try this if the first two options are exhausted.

I highly recommend you rent your garages out for extra revenue. Some landlords even frame a wall down the middle of a double garage, put in a door on both sides for separate access, and then rent out the garage space to two separate tenants. This raises revenues even more.

Not renting the garage for extra means unnecessarily leaving money on the table. I highly recommend you rent your garages.

Raise Revenue – Basement Storage

Additional Revenue Potential: $200-$500 per month

The highest use of a residential property that I've ever heard of was a landlord who rented two suites in a property (upstairs and down), four parking spaces, two separate sides of a garage, and a separate room for storage in a basement that wasn't attached to a suite. Of all these extra income options, renting the basement as storage is probably the least common, but it's nonetheless viable in some circumstances.

The scenario for renting the basement as storage usually arises when there is an unfinished basement with a separate entrance. It's imperative that the entrance be completely separate from the entrance used by the upstairs tenants.

Many landlords will rent a basement for storage when their plan is to eventually convert the basement into an accessory apartment but they're not currently able to for whatever reason. It's a good way to get the upstairs tenant prepared for the change of another tenant in the basement, and it also helps the landlord raise funds for the basement renovation when it happens. Alternatively, the landlord may just keep the basement as a storage rental over the long term.

Other than a separate entrance, the biggest factor to consider with basement storage rentals is that the property must be more appealing than a commercial storage locker space. Keep in mind that commercial storage lockers are very expensive (about $250 per month for less than 200 square feet), so beating the big guys on price shouldn't be that difficult.

Other than price, your basement rental storage space should be bigger than a commercial storage locker, which again shouldn't be that difficult considering the small size of commercial storage lockers.

If you choose to rent out a basement for storage, your biggest customers will be contractors who need a place to store materials. Often they will need this space to save them the hassle of transporting materials over a long distance.

Raise Revenue – Cell Phone Tower

Additional Revenue Potential: $150-$400 per month

Unfortunately, this isn't a source of income that a landlord can actively pursue. A property has to be in an ideal location for the cell phone company to need such a space, and if they do, they will contact you.

I only know of one landlord with a cell phone tower on a building. It's an 18-suite apartment building situated on high ground in Hamilton. The owner purchased the building with the cell phone tower and lease already in place.

Raise Revenue – Advertising Space

Additional Revenue Potential: $200-$1000 per month

Unlike a cell phone tower, the landlord can play a more active role in seeking out income from advertising space. Two major factors must be considered in order to carry out this strategy.

First, your property must be in a high-traffic location. Since many real estate investors avoid high-traffic locations, this will take many properties out of consideration. But if the property *is* in a high traffic location, then you might have an in-demand ad space.

Second, you must find out if local bylaws allow permanent ads to be placed on residential properties. If law allows them, then you must find out if there are any restrictions and abide by those restrictions. These may include the size of the ads and the structural integrity of the building they're being attached to.

Raise Revenue – Use Creativity

As a savvy and committed landlord, there are no limits to the ways you can maximize revenue.

By regularly analyzing your sources of income and seeking ways to raise revenues, you'll find there are many opportunities available to you. In addition to the tried and tested methods discussed above, you will learn unique ways to increase revenues from fellow landlords and even from the properties themselves.

My only caution to creatively thinking about raising revenues is that you always do so under strict moral and legal guidelines, and that you seek to create additional value to your tenants in the process.

"Sometimes we stare so long at a door that is closing that we see too late the one that is open"

— Alexander Graham Bell

Chapter 4

DECREASING EXPENDITURES

Systematic Approach

As with every aspect of landlording, it's best to approach decreasing expenditures systematically. This means regularly looking at expenses and analyzing them while simultaneously looking for ways to be more efficient.

But, how does a proactive landlord turn this process into a system?

This is where a solid financial tracking and bookkeeping system comes into play (we'll discuss these in more details later). Leveraging solid organization in these areas, a proactive landlord will schedule quarterly and annual periods of analysis using financial reports created by a bookkeeper.

As a landlord, you'll see a lot of receipts and regularly deal with different expenses. If you're only managing one or two properties, it might be fairly easy to keep expenses clear in your mind and analyze them while looking for efficiencies. When you start to manage more and more properties, however, it gets more and more difficult to maintain clarity in your own mind. At that point, it's vital that the landlord utilize a system to ensure the analysis is being done with accuracy and in a timely manner.

By examining the quarterly and year-end reports, a landlord is able to see all the expenses listed in a row. This allows the landlord several advantages:

1. **Detecting Abnormalities** – Imagine you have the water bill in your name. Upon seeing three months of water bill expenses side-by-side, you notice the bill skyrocketed by $100 on the third month. This can almost certainly be associated with a leak somewhere on the property.

   This is something the tenant wouldn't likely tell you about unless they suddenly saw water flooding into their home. If it were just a leaky faucet or running toilet, the tenant would likely not mention anything. Only by analyzing the quarterly report would you identify this abnormal expense.

2. **Identifying Excessive Expenses** – By seeing all of your property expenses side-by-side, you will be able to notice excessive costs associated with one property versus the others.

   For example, imagine you own 8 properties each of approximately the same value with approximately 20% equity on each one. Looking at all of your monthly mortgage payments side-by-side, you'll quickly notice if one property has an exorbitantly high mortgage expense. Based on that analysis, you can then appropriately plan to reduce that mortgage expense, whether by refinancing the property or by selling the property if refinance isn't possible. Analyzing your strongly performing properties will help you make appropriate plans for the underperforming properties.

There are no limits to the kinds of efficiencies you'll be able to identify by going through this process. If you don't see it already, you'll soon notice how success in real estate is about letting cumulative effects add up over time—the longer the better, and the larger the accumulation the better. You'll see that small changes applied to multiple properties over time makes for big results. Here are a few more examples of inefficiencies you might discover during the quarterly and annual report analysis period:

1. **Unfair Tax Assessments** – If you discover an inaccurate tax assessment, you can dispute it and pay lower tax if you win the dispute.

2. **Insurance Premiums** – You may discover that you can save money by grouping all of your insurance policies under one provider for a discount.

3. **Hot Water Heaters** – You may notice that a property has a rental hot water heater that could be bought out; this would remove the monthly expense for a hot water heater rental.

4. **Re-Amortization** – Depending on your goal for the property in question and how long you've had the mortgage, you may find that you can re-amortize the mortgage to reduce the mortgage expense on renewal, therefore increasing cash flow. For example, a $200,000 loan (five-year fixed closed mortgage at 3.54%) with a 25-year amortization would have monthly payments of $1002.77. The same mortgage amount with a 30-year amortization would drop your payments to $899.67. The overall interest amount that you pay on the total mortgage would increase because of the longer amortization, but your monthly payments are reduced by $100.

5. **Take Austerity Measures** – Seeing the numbers all in a row gives you the opportunity to acknowledge your expenditures and practice restraint. Perhaps you noticed that at the end of three months, you've spent on average $200 per month at Home Depot. You can now consider whether or not those expenses were necessary or the repair should have been given to a particular contractor.

Perhaps you realize that you reacted to a tenant's complaints precipitously by rushing to the store for an unnecessary quick fix when the job still required a handyman to come repair it afterward. This is wasted money that you should catch with quarterly and year-end analysis.

Skip A Mortgage Payment – This might be an option if your bank allows it. You may want to consider it if your yearly cash flow is low for any reason. This is usually caused by a major repair. Remember, though, that the interest not paid in that skipped month gets tacked onto the mortgage as additional principal, so this strategy isn't good for equity or as an option to exercise regularly.

An Efficient Expenditure Decrease

I regularly analyze each property in my portfolio for efficiencies, but over the course of my investment career, there is one favourite method I've employed to improve cash flow – refinancing. I use refinancing whenever possible to improve the overall numbers. As discussed above, there are several reasons why this can work, but I recently made one small shift that improved the cash flow by $170 per month on one property.

Investors often look for big changes that will result in a homerun, but real estate success is often about small improvements applied across an entire portfolio over a long period of time. Every change for the better multiplies over time. The longer you hold a property with stronger numbers, the more you benefit.

On the property in question, the original mortgage was a mortgage plus improvements mortgage. The bank advanced money initially to purchase the property. They then held a portion in trust for the improvements that we were going to make on the property. Once we completed the improvements, the bank would advance the remainder of the money.

The original mortgage was by no means a bad mortgage. The interest rate was for 3.99%. Traditionally, this would be an incredibly low rate, but in current extreme low interest rate environment, 3.99% is actually quite high. When the mortgage came due, I was able to secure a 2-year mortgage term with an obscenely low 2.59% interest rate.

Excellent investors continually seek to make these kinds of changes to their overall cash flow situation. The example given above probably doesn't seem too dramatic, and you might be thinking, "That's no way to get wealthy," but before you rush to any conclusions, please consider the effect of this small change over a five-year period.

Since my cash flow was already strong before making this small change, I'm now able to use the extra $170 per month for mortgage pay down. This means that over 5 years, I'll be able to pay down an additional $10,200 (12 months x 5 years x $170). Of course, I'll be able to find more efficiencies and ultimately be able to pay down more principle, so the picture will get even better.

Every dollar of mortgage paid amounts to less interest paid over the long haul. Now consider that I've been able to find small efficiencies in every property, not uncommonly in the range of $170. In fact, I'd say my average improvement has been $150 per property every year.

By plugging that entire savings amount into paying my mortgage down, it's as though I'm removing one entire mortgage payment from my monthly expenses.

SECTION 3: POLICIES AND PROCEDURES

"Policies are the tools that support
excellent relationships."

— QUENTIN D'SOUZA

THE MEAT OF THE BOOK

You'll recall from the introductory sections of this book that relationships are the most important aspect of successful landlording. You might also recall that successful relationships are a small part principle and are a large part art. It's up to the individual landlord to apply the principles in his or her unique way to master the art of relationships.

However, the science of landlording is a series of small actions taken at the right time in the right situation. Knowing what to do in any given situation is daunting to new and experienced landlords alike. This book (and this section in particular) is designed to provide you with the right actions to fit each situation. The rest of the book deals with these situation-specific actions.

"If you are not failing every now and again,
it's a sign you are not doing anything very innovative."

— Woody Allen

Chapter 5

POLICIES AS EFFICIENT TOOLS

Policies

Many of the policies in this book have been developed through the time-tested procedure of trial and error, but many of them have been learned from other landlords who have shared their experiences over the years. Unfortunately, I cannot recall exactly who taught me each policy, procedure, or system but wherever possible, I will credit the fellow landlord who taught me. In many cases the information has entered the matrix of my own brain and come out as a policy in my own business policy manual, now being passed on to you through this book. I apologize in advance to any landlord I've failed to mention as the teacher of any specific policy.

It may sound almost robotic or overly businesslike, but whenever I learn something new, I have to write it down into a policy in order to remember it. As a landlord, you'll be learning all the time. Whenever you have a conversation with another landlord or even a tenant, you'll have a chance to learn.

We always say we'll remember, but the truth is that we often forget. That's why I've personally developed the habit of putting effective new knowledge into policy immediately. In this way, I know what to do even when a situation arises for the first time. This is the course of action I recommend for you whether you're an experienced landlord or a new landlord.

The remainder of this section contains policies that are to be used in order for a real estate business to run smoothly. These policies help to set guidelines for employees, business partners, contractors and tenants. They could be posted on your company website and also included in a tenant manual. Some of these policies may be included in the lease as an appendix and may be outlined as rules for the tenants.

POLICIES ARE BORN OUT OF EXPERIENCE

Early in my landlording experience, I made the mistake of being too flexible on my move-out inspection policy. When this came back to haunt me to the tune of $700, I quickly realized that I needed to create a solid policy to remedy the situation.

On that occasion, the tenant was supposed to make some repairs to the property for damage he'd caused. Unfortunately, I didn't get into the suite quickly enough to jointly fill out a proper inspection form, and the tenant vacated the property without making the repairs.

Yes, I would have had legal recourse, although it would have been difficult to win in small claims court without a properly documented paper trail. I eventually decided not to go through the small claims procedure because I estimated that my time was far more valuable spent working than chasing $700. It would have taken me several hours for the small claims procedure, and I was certain that I could never recoup enough money to pay for the cost of my time spent in small claims court.

Based on that costly experience, I implemented a firm inspection policy, discussed below. Since implementation of that policy, I've never had another problem with losing money on unnecessary renovations to remedy tenant-caused damage.

Policies work when you create, implement, and follow them.

"If you don't design your own life plan, chances are you'll fall into someone else's plan. And guess what they have planned for you? Not much."

— Jim Rohn

Chapter 6

ORGANIZATION POLICIES

Office Organization

You will need to keep an office area dedicated to your real estate business in your home. The larger your real estate business the more space you will require. You will definitely need a computer with internet access, a printer (preferably with a scanner/fax feature), a filing cabinet that can hold legal and letter sized folders, and a place to store tools and supplies. This may sound obvious, but you'd be surprised how many landlords don't closely follow this rule.

Your biggest asset for effective management is information. To inform most—if not all—decisions, you must use the correct information. This information will be found in your office, either in your computer files or in a hard copy. When it comes time to use this information, it's imperative that you're able to find this information quickly.

If it takes you 3 hours to find a receipt or a contact number, you're not effectively using your time. Consider how much your time is worth. In the past, I've calculated that my time is worth $135 per hour using my current earning potential at that time. This means that if I spend 3 hours finding a document, I've just wasted $405. It's this kind of frustrating time-waster that causes landlords to give up real estate.

But this problem can be avoided by having a properly organized office. I recall a time last winter when I experienced ice damming in one of my properties. I needed to know immediately whether or not our insurance would cover the damage caused by ice damming. The way to find out my coverage was to call the insurance provider for that property. Without having to search or struggle, I immediately opened up the property binder for the property in question. Within moments, I'd found the number, called the insurance agent, and discovered that damage from ice damming was not covered in my insurance. I knew that I'd have to cover all of the expenses, and was able to quickly find the right contractors to fix the problem. I used money from the reserve fund to pay for the fix.

My office organization didn't stop me from having to pay for the repairs, but it did mean that I could make rapid decisions and remediate the problem in short order without much difficulty. In fact, within 30 minutes of learning of the problem, I already had the repair procedure well underway and was enjoying lunch with my family.

Office organization will help ensure that your entire landlording experience runs smoothly in all kinds of situations.

Special Tip - Wait Time Can Be Useful Time

To be a successful landlord, you must master the art of time-management. One of the most effective ways to do this is to purposefully use wait times. Follow these policies for maximizing wait times:

1. When you are waiting to show a unit or meet a contractor, be sure to bring something to work on.

   This could involve making tenant phone calls, working on property ads, taking pictures, letting in and instructing contractors, or inspecting a property for repairs.

2. Never go to a property immediately (unless it's an emergency) when a tenant calls.

   When you schedule a visit, scan through all the tasks that need to be done from previous visits/tenant reports and do them during one visit.

3. Create a tenant-relationship building procedure.

   Ask your tenants what problems they see arising soon with maintenance or if they have any other concerns with the property.

Business Hours

Setting normal business hours is vital to landlording. You are a businessman or businesswoman. You're not at the whim of tenants or anyone else. You set your hours and others adhere to them:

1. Conduct business and communication during regular business hours from 9 AM to 5 PM from Monday to Friday.

   This helps to set boundaries and manage tenant expectations regarding communication, repairs, and maintenance.

2. Make exceptions to business hours only for emergencies.

   In the event of an emergency 24/7, tenants will be directed to a cell phone number using the voicemail system to be addressed right away. When you receive an emergency notification from the system, it's imperative that you respond immediately.

3. Don't interrupt your life for non-emergency calls.

   Simply deal with the issue at hand at the next available time during regular business hours. I'm not suggesting you keep tenants waiting, but it's key that you don't let your life be dictated by non-emergency tenant concerns.

4. Communicate your schedule for non-emergency problem-solving with tenants from the beginning of the tenancy to set the tone early.

THE IMPORTANCE OF BOUNDARIES

The boundaries you set for your tenants are life boundaries. It's about keeping your life for you, your family, and your friends. Real estate is a business, which means you'll take care of it during business time.

The down side of not setting boundaries is that you will quickly become consumed by tenant concerns and quickly become a high risk for real estate burnout. This is a major cause of real estate investors quitting or just ceasing to acquire more rental properties.

The purpose of this manual is to help you avoid this fate, and setting boundaries is an important component of ensuring this.

Paperwork Filing System

The following policies ensure that a landlord's paperwork system is streamlined and effective.

1. **Use a filing system that separates each property into its own documentation area.**

   Keep all files from each property in a separate expanding file portfolio and label the spine of the portfolio so that it's easy to identify each property.

2. **Divide each portfolio into different sections.**

   Use the same colored folders for each section in each portfolio to make them easy to find. The portfolio should contain the following sections:

   a. Tenant Information – Contact Information, Leases, Applications, Credit Checks.

   b. Bank Account – Year-end print out of account transactions for the year and the cheque books associated with property.

   c. Property Documents – Property Taxes, MPAC, and utility bills when property is vacant

   d. Insurance – All documents related to insurance and warranties.

   e. Monthly Expenses – utility bills, mortgage payment updates, property taxes updates.

3. **Keep a filing cabinet in a separate secure area in which you can house a mortgage and purchase agreement folder (legal size) for each property.**

4. **Use a separate binder to keep track of all tenant communication.**

   This separate binder was discussed earlier in the book. This includes a separate spreadsheet at the front of the binder which will enable you to stay up to date on property inspections, CO_2/smoke detector inspections, dates when post-dated cheques run out, and mortgage renewal dates.

5. **Scan tenant specific materials into the computer when tenancy ends.**

   The paper copies are then placed in a banker's box and stored safely outside of the office. The same applies for properties that are sold after taxes have been completed on the property.

6. **Whenever you get a receipt for a property, write the name of property on the receipt for easy bookkeeping.**

Mail and Deliveries

Your mail policies provide an opportunity to increase your level of professionalism. I recommend providing an office address on the lease and for all mail because it's more professional and authoritative. The following are the policies on mail and deliveries:

1. Set up a UPS mailbox address with a suite number in order to give your business a professional look and feel. UPS will receive all mail and then forward the mail received to your personal address.

2. Provide every tenant with an address on the lease as a service address.

3. Have all mail directed to your office if you have an office address.

Phone System

A well set up phone system is a major key to your ability to be able to manage your time well and set boundaries between your business and personal life.

1. **Use evoice.com or grasshopper.com to create a phone system with prompts that filter tenant requests to different phone lines. Press 1 for one type of problem, press 2 for another etc.**

   Educating your tenants on the difference between types of requests is an important component in getting your filters to work for you. The tenant binder, which will be explained later on, and move-in are wonderful opportunities to do this.

2. **Create a 2nd phone line to deal specifically with maintenance issues.**

   Set this line up so you're not notified directly on your cell phone. Check these messages regularly and respond promptly, but not immediately. However, ensure that you manage tenants' expectations reasonably when it comes to maintenance response times. Once the expectation is set, always respond within the expected response time. I generally provide a response within 24 hours.

3. **Create a 3rd phone line to deal with vacancies.**

   As with the maintenance line, you should not answer this line immediately. Deal with it systematically, but not with emergency priority.

4. **Create a 4th phone line to deal with emergencies.**

   Have these calls forwarded directly to your cell phone. If tenants contact you on this number, it means there is an issue that has to be dealt with immediately, not in a day or two.

5. **Do not have tenants contact you directly by cell phone or text message.**

   Tenant requests can be overwhelming over time, and you don't want to give the appearance that you are buddies with the tenant. Keep a professional relationship at all times. Keeping this boundary firm can be the difference between successful landlording and wanting to throw in the towel. If you are going to use a cell phone to communicate with tenants have a separate phone number that you use for your rental properties.

6. **Put phone numbers on magnets with the name of your company and place it on the fridge when the property is rented out.**

   This allows easy access for tenants to the necessary information and insures they don't forget the correct numbers. Remember to educate them about the proper use of each number and what does and does not constitute an emergency.

"Ask not that the journey be easy;
ask instead that it be worth it."

— John F Kennedy

Chapter 7

COMMUNICATION POLICIES

Policy on Communication

Landlord-tenant relationships are back-and-forth by nature. There will always be times when you need to work together with your tenant in order for everyone to achieve the result they desire.

The reality is that tenants will not always be perfectly civil and helpful. I'm not suggesting that tenants are irresponsible and unkind. They are like any other sector of society; there are great people and some who are less helpful. You can't always control your tenants' behaviour or whether or not they'll be civil and kind, but you can control yourself.

When a stressful situation arises, it's essential that you act as the leader. A leaky roof, flooded basement, or broken down furnace isn't fun for anyone, especially your tenant. At moments like these, the tenant really needs you to be the leader.

There's probably no more important time to follow the policy to the letter than in your communication. How you communicate with your tenant is in many ways the most important aspect of being an effective and successful landlord.

None of your other policies will be useful if your communications policies aren't right or not carried out properly. A tenant is in many ways a landlord's partner. Without his or her help and participation, the job of landlording is very difficult. Your way of communicating with tenants can be the distinction between excellent and mediocre landlording .

The following is a list of best communication policies:

1. Keep communications professional at all times. Even if tenants are grouchy or annoying, don't snap back at them. Always take the high road and focus all of your energy on getting what you need done.

2. Keep the lines of communication open with tenants. Be proactive and perform preventative communication. Knowing about any property-related issues before going to the property will help save hours of time. It will allow you to prepare contractors and materials in a timely manner.

3. Do not become buddies with tenants; however, aside from official notices, you can use a relaxed tone in your communication. There's nothing wrong with taking an interest in tenants' life or making small talk, but becoming friends with a tenants opens the door to them taking rules for granted.

4. When you have a contractor make a repair, follow up with the tenant to be sure the problem has been fixed. Also ensure that the work has been done neatly. This is the landlording equivalent of excellent customer service. If you do this, your tenants will understand that you actually care about the property and their experience living there.

5. Keep tenants informed about the neighborhood or about building items that might impact them. For example, inform them of garbage pickup changes, parades, or neighborhood garage sales. This helps the tenants take better care of your assets and impresses upon them that you run a tight ship.

6. Offer tenants a finder's fee if a tenant they recommend is accepted in one of your vacant properties. This is one avenue of advertising upcoming vacancies, and also beneficial to you to have endorsed tenants moving into your other properties; it creates a community feel.

7. Initiate communication with your tenants—even about something minor— if no contact has occurred with them in six months.

8. Give holiday cards to tenants thanking them.

9. If managing a larger building, consider putting together a quarterly or semiannual newsletter giving specific information related to the properties in the neighborhood. You can use the newsletter to educate your tenants on the benefits of leasing in your building.

10. Use a tenant survey to gain information on how you're doing as a landlord and how to improve your property and the services that you offer. Keep surveys short—between five and seven questions—and use yes/no or multiple-choice questions. This will greatly increase the chance of the survey being completed. Find out which features tenants like best about the property and get an idea of their satisfaction level. Use this information to improve your landlording operation.

11. Make sure when you're communicating with tenants that you include as many details as possible about repairs, maintenance, and upcoming work. This will ensure tenants don't come back to you with questions regarding the work to be completed. It helps them to feel a part of the process.

12. Provide new tenants with a positive company slogan. For example, I use "We provide a quality home, a safe home, and excellent service" as our slogan.

13. Purchase and use a stamp on all mail correspondence that says something to the effect of, "Our Tenants Are Great!"

If you look at all the different communication policies above, you may start to surmise that every aspect of landlording is affected by proper communications. Let's take a closer look at the ways proper communication simplifies a landlord's job:

1. **Occupancy** – By involving your tenants in the process when a vacancy comes up, you're more likely to fill vacancies with friends and family of existing tenants.

2. **Simplified Maintenance** – By openly communicating with tenants about inspections and speaking to them in advance of inspections, you can enroll tenants in the job of maintaining your property.

3. **Mitigate Tenant Damage** – By clearly informing a tenant of his or her role in caring for the home, you'll find that tenant-related damage is reduced.

4. **Property Care** – In addition to educating tenants on how to minimize damage, it's also our job as landlords to educate tenants on proper care of the property. This can mean seasonal yard maintenance, turning off outdoor faucets before winter, cleaning, and any number of property care aspects.

5. **Tenant Complaints** – By working openly *with* tenants rather than taking an adversarial approach, you'll find that tenants are less likely to angrily complain and more likely to work with you when a problem arises.

6. **Fewer Calls** – Since you'll be expending significant effort educating tenants, your phone system will receive fewer calls overall. The more knowledgeable your tenants are about their responsibilities, and the more proactive you are about any property concerns, the fewer calls from tenants you'll get asking you to take care of issues.

Policy on Phone Communication and Messages

The phone is an important tool in your landlording communication strategy, but don't allow yourself to be a hostage to the phone. These policies are designed for effectiveness and efficiency:

1. **Batch as many phone calls to tenants at the same time each day in order to get the most accomplished.**

2. **Use the phone as the second mode of communication and email as the first.**

   This allows you to keep an electronic record of communication. It's important to have records because you must be able to demonstrate your communication. If anything were to go wrong, you have your emails to print and bring to the Landlord-Tenant board. It would be impossible to provide proof with phone conversations.

3. **Periodically, make random phone calls to tenants to find out if there's anything that you can help with or any problem that you can correct.**

These phone calls will allow the landlord to get a good sense of when vacancies will be arising and what renovations and fixes will be upcoming.

I tend to make my 'random' calls just before my spring and fall inspections so that I can prepare tradespeople in advance. Once I'm aware of the repair issues, I bring the tradesperson with me to the inspection, which is more efficient than making a second trip to the property for repairs.

The calls let your tenants know that you're keeping an eye on the property, and that you're there to ensure their tenancy is as comfortable as possible.

4. **Keep phone conversations professional.**

As with the general communication policies (see below), don't be the tenant's buddy during phone conversations. You may choose to be more casual, but stick the point in order to get your job done.

Policy on Property Binder

As mentioned above, each unit should have its own binder that contains key information regarding the property. This is referred to as the tenant binder in other parts of the book. Here are the policies that govern the property/tenant binders:

1. **Use a white one-inch 3-ring binder.**

2. **These binders remain in the property at all times.**

3. **Educate the tenant about everything in the tenant binder at the end of the move-in inspection.**

Use this as an opportunity to create a relationship with the tenant and show how proactive you are as a landlord. Explain that the tenant binder is a friend of both tenant and landlord because it has the answer to many problems. If used properly, the binder can save much time for all involved, so being knowledgeable about it is imperative.

See **www.theontariolandlordtoolbox.ca** for a Sample Property Binder.

Here is a sample of the Table of Contents from a property binder.

Policy on Computer Information and Email

As mentioned above, email is the preferred method of communication because it allows you to keep a record of every action taken. Knowing that you're compiling data in case it's ever needed, you can control the flow of communication and prove your willingness to resolve issues and follow steps mutually agreed upon.

Please take your data seriously. These policies are designed to ensure that your data is safe, well organized, and useful if it is ever needed as proof in a landlord-tenant dispute:

1. **Ensure that each folder on your computer that includes property-specific information is subdivided by the address of the property.**

    This will help make sure that information can be accessed quickly.

2. **Back up data and email archives stored on a local computer in two locations that are separate from the computer.**

One location can be a portable hard-drive, and the other location should be a secure cloud storage service like Dropbox or Google Drive. This redundancy ensures you don't ever lose your data— costly to a landlord.

3. **Ensure all e-mail records are kept.**

   This is your proof in case a dispute ever arises. Knowing that you're compiling proof, be sure that *all* of your communications are professional, thorough, and proactive.

4. **Include a signature at the bottom of every e-mail message and be sure that the date can easily be identified.**

   This is important to developing a proof trail.

5. **Always use the same e-mail address to send messages to tenants. Keep your personal and business emails separate.**

THE VALUE OF DATA

Having redundancies in your data system is critically important. Imagine it's late November or early December and suddenly your computer crashes, erasing all of your files. Without having redundancy for your files, you're immediately going to have a big problem managing your real estate business.

The first thing you'll quickly realize is that all of your year's bookkeeping is suddenly gone. On a portfolio of 5-10 properties, you'll suddenly be on the hook for thousands of dollars of bookkeeping fees just to get your books back in order. The extra cost of not backing up files is bad enough, but the pain of time wasted will be even worse.

Losing a paper trail for a problem tenant could be even more costly. Remember that if you ever have to take a tenant to the Landlord Tenant Board to force an eviction. It's vital that you have a paper trail of all events leading up to the eviction. Keeping detailed notes and email records of all the communications that have taken place will be vital to your chances of an eviction going your way.

To avoid this fate, take the simple and relatively inexpensive step of backing up all of your files with an external hard drive and cloud storage. If you ever lose your data, you'll certainly find the cost of backing it up to be vastly less expensive.

New Management of Rental Property

Use these policies for transferring a new rental property to new management:

1. Use a letter informing the tenants of new management and your role. Let the tenants know about your win-win policies.

2. Get a copy each tenants' rental agreement as well as a list of all current deposits on file.

3. Obtain a rental history for each property from the previous owner.

4. Ensure that you visit the property within the first week of taking over management.

5. Take care of any major maintenance issues immediately. Let the tenants know the time frame of the repairs.

6. Address the tenants' most important concerns.

7. Provide the tenants with your contact information.

"You don't have to see the top of the staircase
to take the first step."

— Martin Luther King

Chapter 8

FUNDS AND LATE RENT POLICIES

Policy on Reserve Funds

A reserve fund is used to cover regular and emergency expenses for a particular property. There are several keys to the reserve fund policy:

1. **Amount** - I like to see at least three times the gross monthly expenses in each property account.

2. **Timing** – It's imperative to start with the reserve fund from the beginning. It's important that you start ownership of the property with a full reserve fund and don't wait to build up the fund with cash flow, regardless of how strong the cash flow is. It's always at the most inopportune moment when you're hit with a big expense. You never know when you're going to need a reserve fund. If you can't afford it, you can't afford to own the property. It's that simple.

If you're purchasing the property with a joint venture money partner, ensure they understand the reserve fund is their responsibility.

3. **Leverage Last Month's Rent** – I utilize the last month's rent as part of the reserve fund in each account. This reduces some of the pressure of raising the full amount.

4. **Allow For Upcoming Capital Expenditures** – The rule to have three times your monthly expenses in the reserve fund only applies to unknown expenditures. Do a serious and thorough analysis of real upcoming capital expenses and be sure that the reserve fund has the money to cover them. If the roof has to be done soon, make sure there is enough to do the roof. There's no excuse for being surprised by large capital expenditures.

Policy on Funds

Tracking funds is an essential component of effective landlording. Without concise tracking, you can't have concise bookkeeping. Concise bookkeeping allows landlords to analyze expenses and income effectively and also reduce expenses and add income.

Concise tracking is essential if Canada Revenue Agency (CRA) ever chooses to audit your business. Joint venture partners also appreciate when all funds are tracked accurately. It creates a level of trust that otherwise wouldn't exist between joint venture partners.

The following is a rundown of essential policies on funds and tracking of funds:

1. **Track all funds, whether paid or received.**

2. **Write which property is associated with the expense directly on the receipt.**

Make a small note if it was paid with cash. If paid by credit card, the receipt will indicate this.

3. **Pay by cheque whenever possible.**

   The cheque acts as a built-in receipt. If a contractor fails to provide an invoice, you will still have proof of payment that you can use for tracking expenses.

4. **When issuing a cheque for a contractor, photocopy the cheque and attach it to the invoice.**

5. **Always pay contractors within 24 hours of the completion of work.**

   This creates strong relationships with contractors. They will quickly remember you as a customer who pays bills quickly and will make your jobs a priority in the future.

6. **Photocopy and keep on record each post-dated cheque when received.**

7. **Keep a separate bank account for each property.**

   This makes it easy to keep track of rents and expenses. As you build your property empire, it will be easier to manage your accounts with each property in a separate account.

Policy on Rent Collection

As your number of rental properties increases, one of the challenges you will have is dealing with rent collection. This includes the need to deposit a large number of cheques. There are many ways to collect rent, but there are only a few really efficient methods of doing it.

1. **Going To the Door** - If you're just starting out and have one tenant, it might be okay to go to pick up the rent just to get your feet wet. But you should know that it's the *tenant's* responsibility to pay you rent and pay it on time. They should be delivering it to you at your place of business— within business hours and on time. You really shouldn't go to collect rent from a tenant as this isn't a good use of your time and promotes bad habits.

2. **Post-Dated Cheques** - As a convenience, offer your tenants the ability to pay you using postdated cheques. What you can then do on the banking side is take envelopes from your bank's ATM and prepare your cheques for deposit beforehand. You can write the amount and the account number on the outside of the envelope that you are depositing at the ATM. When you go to the bank the next morning, you can simply put the cheque in the envelope with the right account and amount. Still, the process of preparing the cheques and depositing them takes time. But this procedure can save you a lot of time and is better than taking a stack of cheques to the ATM and trying to deposit them or going into a branch and doing the same thing.

3. **Cheque Cashing Bank Services** - Some banks offer you the opportunity to provide them with your postdated cheques, and they, in turn, will deposit them for you. I've never been charged for using the service, and it can be quite handy. There are banks that do charge for this, so shop around a bit if you plan to use this strategy. The negative issue is that it doesn't offer you the flexibility that you may need when you're working with tenants. You may be required to hold off depositing a cheque for 24 hours, and this service might not allow you the time to do that.

4. **Online Payment Systems** - There are quite a few services, such as TenantPay.com, that offer online bill payment systems. The company offers your tenants a way to pay you rent just like they pay online bills. They would basically put in TenantPay as the payee and then enter the TenantPay account number that you give them. When they pay, the money goes directly into your account within 24 hours. This is a great option compared to cheques. A NSF cheque can take five or six business days come back, but a tenant could not even make the payment on TenantPay if they didn't have the funds in their account. One big drawback for me is that you are dependent on the tenant to pay their rent on time using the online bill payment feature, and you could potentially have payments coming in at all different times of the day and night. Depending on the type of tenants that you have, this might be a great or not-so-great feature. The cost of this service is based on the volume of your monthly transactions. It becomes more cost-effective the more transactions that you do.

5. **eTransfers** – These payments are also known as email money transfers. The money goes directly into your bank account immediately. This is almost like getting a cash rent payment, except that you have an electronic paper trail. A tenant uses this service through their bank. The fee is paid by the tenant, not the landlord, another benefit of using eTransfers. Just like online payment systems, the big drawback is that you are dependent on the tenant to initiate the rent payment process.

6. **Pre-Authorized Debits** – This is another payment service offered through most of the major banks, like the Royal Bank of Canada. You set up a business account with the

bank with the ability to do Pre-Approved Deposits and Pre-Approved Payments. This allows you to create a pre-authorized debit (PAD) for each tenant. The tenant fills out a simple agreement and provides a voided check. You complete an electronic file at the end of the month and upload it to your bank and then the bank goes into each Tenants Account, takes the money out, and puts it directly in your bank account. Again, you know immediately which tenants, if any, are not able to pay. I am the one who is initiating the payment process, so I'm not depending on the tenants to do it. This service costs a flat fee of approximately $50 a month.

NSF Cheques

You may run into the case where you believe a cheque is going to be NSF (non-sufficient funds). There are some policies I use to deal with this situation, but for them to be most effective, you need to go to the bank location listed on the cheque.

1. **Take the check to the issuing bank to see if it'll clear.**

   If you have an account with that bank, it makes the process much easier. You simply go to a bank teller, show them the cheque, and ask them if the cheque will clear. If it does, deposit the check immediately.

2. **Another strategy is to take a cheque from a tenant and certify it.**

   Instead of cashing the cheque, you can just go to the issuing bank and ask them to certify the cheque. Usually there's a charge of around $20. This can be useful especially when you're dealing with a problem tenant who's moving out.

Screening for Bounced Cheques

If a cheque bounces, it's important that you know immediately. Follow these policies to stay proactive:

1. **Check your account for bounced cheques 3-4 days after the cheque has been deposited. Do this for 10 business days.**

2. **If the cheque bounces:**

   a. Take note of the date the cheque bounced and the bank fees of the returned cheques

   b. Begin the process for dealing with "**Late Rent**."

Late Rent Payment

In my early days as a landlord, I wasn't vigilant enough about rent payments (on a couple of occasions). The gravest example was the time I believed a tenant's promise to pay me late. In fact, I didn't start the correct process for evicting the tenant until about 3 months had passed and he'd issued 3 bounced cheques.

At that point, I finally issued the N4. As we'll discuss below, a landlord must wait 14 days from the issuance of the N4 before he or she can get a date with a Landlord Tenant Board adjudicator (who makes a ruling).

It was the 4th month without any rent received when I finally got the tenant into the Landlord Tenant Board, and it wasn't until the 5th month that I finally had him out of the property.

At the time, I wasn't thinking clearly or treating it like a business. The tenant had three children, one of whom was disabled, and I was thinking like a father rather than a landlord. Of course, there is nothing wrong with compassion. I hope all of the readers of this book act with compassion in life, but I strongly recommend you treat tenant dealings like a business. This means *always* following the process that leads to regularly receiving income for the property. There are other avenues for struggling tenants to receive help – you giving them a break on rent isn't one of the avenues you should consider for helping people.

I learned from that experience how important the proper procedure is when it comes to dealing with late rent. Today, I stick to my policies without exception. Each step of the process is governed by the timeline events. The following are the correct processes and policies for dealing with late rent payment:

1. **Send an email/letter and call within the first 24 hours after rent is late.**

   Below you will find a sample of this letter. This letter is important because if you need to evict, you'll need to prove that you made every effort to solve the issue before going to the Landlord Tenant Board.

2. **In the letter and on the phone, inform tenants they must bring to your place of business a certified cheque, money order, or cash within 24 hours. Otherwise, the paperwork will be started.**

   Never hold up the issuance of an N4 on a promise by the tenant. Waiting to issue the N4 will only slow the process of eviction later if you need to go through that process.

3. **When speaking to the tenant on the phone, explain that you're obliged by best business practice to file the N4**

   Say something like, "My partner would kill me if I didn't follow the process and issue an N4" or "As I explained before you moved in, we follow this N4 process when rent is not received on the due date."

It shows the tenant you're a serious businessperson who follows the procedure without fail.

4. **If tenant provides cash, take a witness and have the tenant sign the rent receipt.**

5. **If the cheque bounces, apply an administration fee of $20 + cost of bank fees.** Charging an outrageous administration fee is an amateur move that will never be held up by the Landlord Tenant Board.

6. **Start a Transaction Summary and keep it up to date. This can include NSF fees and L1 application charges.**

   This is necessary as it later provides proof to the Landlord Tenant Board of monies owed you. By having all the numbers well organized, the adjudicator will easily be able to understand your case. It provides a superior level of organization.

   This is a sample of what it could look like:

Month	Transaction	Paid	Owed
January	Rent		- $1500
January	Bounced Cheque		- $20+$8=$28
January	LTB Filing Fee		- $170
February	Rent	$500	- $1500
Sub-Total		$500	- $3198
Total			- $2198

7. **Collect all past and current communication between tenant, property manager, and landlord.**

   This means emails, maintenance request forms, and written communication. Also collect any new communication between landlord, property manager, and tenant. If this goes to Landlord Tenant Board, you will need to have three copies of each document, but a single copy is fine for now.

8. **If the problem is not rectified within 24 hours, give an N4 accompanied by a personable letter in plain English.**

   N4 must be completed accurately or it will cause the eviction process to fail.

   If the rent is only a day or two late, issue the N4 to protect yourself in the event that the rent is not paid. Do this even if you agree to receive the rent late.

   Explain to the tenant that the N4 is standard business practice, and if they pay the rent before the date on the form (two weeks from the date of the N4), they have nothing to worry about.

9. **Follow this N4 checklist:**

   a. N4 termination date must be no earlier than 14 days after the day the notice was served. Always add an extra day to be sure. (If serving by mail, 5 days must be added). Getting this wrong could mean having to re-file the N4.

   b. The N4 mustn't include anything other than rent. Never add other costs owed to you (NSF fees, administrative charges).

   c. List all tenants named on the lease.

   d. Be accurate – amount, dates, and addresses. Double check!

e. Never withdraw an application on a tenant's promise of payment. Only withdraw the application when certified funds are actually received and cleared.

Failing to get any of these steps right could mean voiding your N4 application, resulting in you having to re-apply for the N4. This can be extremely costly as it effectively moves the eventual eviction date back several weeks, meaning you go longer without receiving rental income.

If you are unsure about this document or its delivery in any way, it is best to use a paralegal or lawyer that specializes in Landlord and Tenant matters to help you complete it correctly.

I've provided two sample letters below that you can use to model your own late rent payment letter on:

Date: June 28th, 20XX
Mr. Thomas Tenant, 222 Maple Street
Whitby, Ontario, B2B 2B2

Dear Mr. Tenant:

As you are already aware, the obligations of your lease require that you pay your rent monthly. Your rent is due on the first day of every month and is late on the second day of the month.

We have not received payment for the current month's rent. As we mentioned in our discussion prior to signing the lease, we have a zero tolerance policy for late rent and are issuing an N4 (Notice to End a Tenancy Early for Non-payment of Rent).

The Residential Tenancies Act states the following if notice is not given in accordance with the Act:

Non-Payment of Rent

---

59. (1) If a tenant fails to pay rent lawfully owing under a tenancy agreement, the landlord may give the tenant notice of termination of the tenancy effective not earlier than,

(a) the 7th day after the notice is given, in the case of a daily or weekly tenancy; and

(b) the 14th day after the notice is given, in all other cases. 2006, c. 17, s. 59 (1).

Please follow the instructions on the N4 document.

You can pay the rent by in person by calling 555-555-5555 and dropping off the rent to 111 Oak Street Whitby, Ontario, A1A 1A1.

Sincerely,

Name of Landlord

Alternatively, you can use a letter more like this one:

Date: June 28th, 20XX

Mr. Thomas Tenant, 222 Maple Street,
Whitby, Ontario, B2B 2B2

Dear Mr. Tenant:

Please be advised that we have a zero tolerance for late rent. Upon tenancy, you were advised that rent is due and payable, in full, on the 1st of the month. Failing to pay rent on time results in the attached N4 - Notice to End a Tenancy Early for Non-payment of Rent.

Please be advised that this document clearly states that full payment within the time stipulated will void this Notice. However, repeated failure to pay will result in an additional notice N8 - Notice to Terminate, which cannot be voided on payment of rent and allows us to continue with the process to evict.

We appreciate your immediate co-operation in this matter.

Sincerely,

Name of Landlord

Delivery of N4

Whenever you start dealing with official notices required by the Landlord Tenant Board, it's imperative to follow process correctly. Follow these policies for successful delivery of an N4:

1. **Never post an N4 on a tenant's door.**

2. **Hand Delivery is the preferred method for delivering an N4.**

   If the N4 is hand delivered, it should have a witness, especially if the tenant is belligerent or ignores communication.

   If the N4 is placed in the tenant's mailbox or in between the screen door and door, take a picture of the N4 in the mailbox or location it was placed. Then take a few steps back and take another picture that shows the mailbox with the house number on it. This should be printed and kept with other communications.

3. **Delivery by courier is the second best method of delivery.**

   If it's impractical to deliver by hand and you choose a courier, do not have the tenant sign for mail, but have the courier note the delivery time. And get a copy of the receipt.

4. **Landlord Tenant Board – Certificate of Service**

   This is held by the landlord for the LTB. The tenant does not get a copy. Please keep a copy in the communication folder. This will be submitted with N4 for filing purposes.

The **Certificate of Service** is found on the Landlord and Tenant Board web site (http://www.ltb.gov.on.ca/). It is basically a form that states you did give a notice or form to a particular person, in a particular way, on a specified date. It is an offence under the Residential Tenancies Act to file false or misleading information with the Landlord and Tenant Board. This certificate must be completed when you serve any notices or forms to tenants.

Following the Issuance of the N4

There are three scenarios that can follow from the issuance of an N4. Below are the policies governing the scenarios along with their correct follow up action:

1. **If tenant pays by specified date in certified funds, take no action – but keep copy of form on file.**

2. **If tenant moves out by that date, you will need to rent it out again – see Filling Vacancies Binder for correct actions to take.**

3. **On the 14th day from issuance of the N4, go to Service Ontario to file the N4, Certificate of Service, and L1.**

   The laws of Ontario essentially allow a tenant to be 14 days late on rent. If the tenant pays within 14 days of your issuing the N4, there is no further action you can take. However, if the tenant doesn't pay, it's important that you proceed with the eviction process correctly.

   You must file three documents with the Landlord Tenant Board (at Service Ontario) at the same time. These are the N4, the Certificate of Service and the L1, which is an application for the end of the tenancy based on non-payment of rent.

   Once you file the L1, you'll be going to the adjudicator with the Landlord Tenant Board to resolve the issue.

4. **Hire a collection agency to collect rent, NSF fees, and filing fees owed.**

   Some reputable collection agencies are *Excel*, and *Credit Control Services*. Remember that tenants are responsible for the fees you've been forced to pay for the eviction process.

This includes NSF fees and the fees you have to pay with the Landlord Tenancy Board for any filings (e.g., N4 and L1, which are each $170).

Persistent Late Payments

When a tenant pays rent every time, but consistently pays late, it's problematic for the landlord as you end up regularly filing an N4. If tenants habitually pay late, it may be nothing more than a poor habit on their part. As a landlord, there are a couple different strategies you can use for consistently late-paying tenants:

1. **If it's the middle of a rental term and you want the tenant out, collect a few N4 notices along with detailed notes; then file an N8 to end the tenancy at the end of the rental term.**

   If the resident decides to fight the tenancy termination and does not move out, you then file an L1 application to terminate the tenancy.

2. **If you have a tenant that has more than one late payment in a calendar year you can use the L9 Form instead of the N4.**

   An L9 is best used as a disincentive that promotes tenant re-education.

   The L9 form can be filed the day after the rent payment was due with the Landlord Tenant Board instead of waiting 14 days (as with the N4) and costs $170.

   The tenant then needs to pay rent owed + NSF fees (if any) + $170 in order to avoid going to the landlord tenant board. This financial disincentive can help to keep the residents rent payments on track because they'll have to pay approximately $200 extra (NSF fees and L9 filing fee) on top of rent when you file an L9 (which could be every time they pay late). This often helps teach the tenant to pay rent on time.

4. **Move to Start the Eviction Process.**

If the tenant fails to pay after either of the above processes, it's time to begin the eviction process.

Cash for Keys

Sometimes it makes more sense to just pay a tenant to leave rather than go through the entire eviction process. Some would argue that by paying a tenant to leave, you are reinforcing a bad habit and not allowing the Landlord and Tenant Board process to do its job. It's great to be able to think with a higher purpose, but I'm running a real estate business, and if I want to be able to continue to run my business, I need to get a non-paying tenant out as quickly as possible.

If I have to have a tenant leave at the end of the month by signing an N11 with a moving incentive and not have to pay for someone to live in a property for 2-3 months while I go through the eviction process, I will do it every single time. A moving incentive could be a couple hundred dollars to cover "moving expenses", or perhaps not paying a month's rent.

An N11 is found on the Landlord and Tenant Board web site (http://www.ltb.gov.on.ca/). It is basically an agreement between the Landlord and the Tenant to end the tenancy early. When a landlord and tenant sign this form, they agree that the tenant will move out by the date on the form. If they do not move out by that date, a Landlord may apply to the Landlord and Tenant Board for an order to evict the tenant without further notice or the need to go to a hearing.

My preference is to do this verbally. If you are not comfortable with this process, you could use a letter that states your intentions. Just make sure that you are there with the N11 in hand. The key is to have the N11 signed and witnessed by someone. You should also remember that any monies are paid once the tenant has actually left the property, or you could accept half of the payment once the N11 is signed and the other half once the tenants have left. You might also include in your agreement the need for the property to be left in good condition.

Here is what a letter might look like:

Date: June 28th, 20XX
Mr. Thomas Tenant, 222 Maple Street
Whitby, Ontario, B2B 2B2

Dear Mr. Tenant:

You are $XXX behind in your rent payments, and we have already filed for a hearing with the Landlord Tenant Board. We understand this process well and will go through with the hearing process, followed with sheriff if necessary, and then to small claims court in order to be paid in full.

We are offering a $XXX incentive to end the tenancy on August 20th, 20XX when tenants (Name of Tenant and Name of Tenant) both vacate Address of Rental Unit (Description of Rental Unit) on or before August 20th at 5pm. This offer will become null and invalid should the tenants vacate the apartment any time after 5pm August 31st.

The following conditions should be met:

1. Signed N11 notice that is attached.
2. Tenant will leave the unit in clean condition (in particular, leave no personal belongings and garbage behind) and hand in the keys.

This is a one-time offer to help you to locate to another residence by

Should you have any questions please feel free to contact me at (877) XXX-XXXX

Thanks,

Name of Landlord

Post-Dated Cheques Have Run Out

Follow these policies if a tenant's post-dated cheques have run out.

1. **Provide a letter or email 30 days before the post-dated cheques are going to run out.**

   Please note that you can't require tenants to pay by post-dated cheques. Both parties must agree on the payment method. However, a tenant should not switch payment method without mutual agreement.

   Here's a sample letter you may use if post-dated cheques run out:

Date: June 28th, 20XX

Mr. Thomas Tenant, 222 Maple Street,
Whitby, Ontario, B2B 2B2

Dear Mr. Tenant:

I hope you are enjoying the nice weather we've been having lately.

I wanted to let you know that I will need new cheques for you, as I only have cheques to cover through July 1st, 20XX. For your convenience, please provide me with new post-dated cheques from August 1st, 20XX on and mail them to me. I would appreciate it greatly. If you aren't able to mail them, I can arrange a time to come by and pick them up. Just let me know.

Please make cheques payable to:

Name of Landlord

111 Oak Street, Whitby, Ontario, A1A 1A1.

The amount of monthly rent on the cheque should be: $1500

Thanks,

Name of Landlord

Send the following letter if no post-dated cheques have been provided within two-weeks of when the cheques have run-out:

Date: July 12th, 20XX

Mr. Thomas Tenant,222 Maple Street

Whitby, Ontario,B2B 2B2

Dear Mr. Tenant:

I wanted to follow up on the request for post-dated cheques sent on June 28th, 20XX.

If you do not wish to pay by post-dated cheques, then it is your responsibility to have the payment submitted in an acceptable method of payment that we mutually agree upon on or before the last day of the month.

59. (1) If a tenant fails to pay rent lawfully owing under a tenancy agreement, the landlord may give the tenant notice of termination of the tenancy effective not earlier than,

  a. the 7th day after the notice is given, in the case of a daily or weekly tenancy; and

  b. the 14th day after the notice is given, in all other cases. 2006, c. 17, s. 59 (1).

As stated in the Residential Tenancies Act:

Non-payment of Rent

Please make payments payable to:

Name of Landlord,

111 Oak Street,, Whitby, Ontario,, A1A 1A1

The amount of monthly rent on the cheque should be $1500.

Sincerely,

Name of Landlord

Receipts and Invoices

Use the following policies for receipts and invoices:

1. Arrange a specific time twice a month to pay all bills.

   One of the two should be a week after rents are deposited.

2. Pay contractors as soon as they give invoices as it shows that you respect the work they d0, and they know they will get paid right away

3. Indicate on your receipts what purchases apply to which property.

   Make sure you write the note immediately when you make the purchase.

4. Keep good notes on repairs from each contractor.

5. Request a receipt for each property separately. This greatly aids in your bookkeeping.

6. Use a high-speed scanner to digitize a copy of the receipts and file them on your computer at the end of each month.

7. Make a photocopy of cheques when received and staple to the receipt.

8. Put all the receipts for each month in a separate envelope. On the front of the envelope, write a summary for each receipt from the store/contractor and the total charge on separate lines.

Bookkeeping Procedures

Follow these policies for bookkeeping:

1. Have a separate bank account for each property.

   This makes it easy to track transactions and identify bounced cheques associated with a particular property.

2. Scan and store receipts and invoices electronically once they come in.

   I like to do this each week, but it's imperative to do it at least every month. Waiting longer than a month increases the likelihood that you'll end up inputting thousands of receipts at year-end.

3. If you are using a separate bookkeeping service, you can easily send your invoices and receipts to that service.

   Use QuickBooks or similar software to manage the bookkeeping for the properties, or use a professional bookkeeper.

   QuickBooks allows you to print monthly, quarterly, and year end reports on each property.

   These are vital to identifying property issues and for reporting to joint venture partners. Be sure to print profit/loss reports as well as reports relating to revenue and expenses.

4. Look at your expenses and revenues for each property at the end of each year and try to identify adjustments to improve your cash flow.

   Keep in mind large capital expenditures associated with each property; this may mean additional reserve funds must be set aside.

5. If you've never used QuickBooks before, I recommend you using Accountant-In-a-Box to learn how to apply QuickBooks to you real estate business. http://accountantinabox.ca/

   This educational resource is efficient at helping you get started quickly.

6. Understand that expense items are tax deductible so be sure to account for them. This is like putting more money in your pocket.

7. Know the difference between a repair and an improvement.

   You want to claim a repair whenever you can. Repairs are treated as an expense in your accounting and are deductible from your tax expenses. George Dube's excellent book _Legal, Tax and Accounting Strategies for the Canadian Real Estate Investor_ covers this topic in detail. I recommend reading this book to gain a strong understanding of real estate accounting, especially the distinction between repairs and improvements.

"Long-range planning works best in the short term."

— Doug Evelyn

Chapter 9

MAINTENANCE, RENOVATION, REPAIR, INSPECTION, AND PROPERTY CARE POLICIES

Policy on Smoking

Smoking rules are simple; it's not allowed in any rental properties. This must be mentioned in the property rules section of the lease. What follows are the basic policies on smoking:

1. Keep properties smoke-free.

   If tenants or guests are going to smoke, insist they smoke outside. Ensure that tenants understand and sign off on the condo bylaws with regards to condominium units.

2. Post no-smoking signs in multi-unit properties.

3. Communicate the difficulty and cost of smoke remediation to tenants. Explain to them that a smoke smell in carpets, drapery, and walls is very difficult remove and any cleaning will be charged back to them.

You should pass on the message that if a tenant breaks the rule, the landlord must undertake smoke remediation immediately, which is a four to six step process:

1. Clean Furnace Ducts – This costs approximately $400

2. Ozone Machine Rental – Used to remediate smells in a house. ($100/day)

3. Replace Furnace Filters – This costs approximately $25

4. Clean Carpets – This costs between $200-$500 depending on how much carpet is in the property.

5. Paint Walls – This costs between $1200-$3000, depending on the size of the property.

6. Paint Ceilings – This costs between $350-$700 depending on the size of the property and the ceiling finishing, but is not always necessary.

7. Replace Carpets – This is only necessary in extreme cases and costs between $600-$2000, depending on the property.

As you can see, the cost to remediate smoke is high. If a tenant smokes in the house, *they must pay* for remediation. The lease will state this, and if a tenant does smoke, I recommend being firm with them. Explain that you have legal recourse to recover the funds needed to remediate the smell of smoke. Legal precedent has been set on this in Ontario. Explain to tenants that this is an issue you'd take to small claims court if necessary.

1. In the unfortunate event that a tenant does break the smoking rule, there are four possible scenarios. Below they're listed from most preferable to least preferable:

2. Tenant Remediates on Their Own – It's the tenant's job to remove the smell of smoke from the property if they smoke in the property. If you find out that a tenant has been smoking, explain to them that this is their responsibility.

3. Tenant Pays – If for any reason a tenant doesn't remediate the smoke smell on their own, you must secure funds from them in order to carry out the remediation yourself. This is obviously not preferable over the first scenario.

Tenant Refuses to Pay Any Compensation – This is the worst-case scenario. If this happens, you will be forced to take the tenant to small claims court to recoup your money. This is one scenario where the process of small claims court would probably be worthwhile since the cost associated with remediating the smell of smoke is so high.

Policy on Pets

When you are first putting a tenant into a property you can disallow a tenancy based on the pet, but once the tenant is in place they are able to bring in pets. In general, it's never really the pet that's the problem, but how the pet owner takes care of the pet. This is true for all sizes of pets. The following are policies to follow for pets:

1. **Small cats and dogs are okay in most properties.**

   The tenant must be responsible for this to work.

2. **All tenants with a pet must sign the pet liability amendment in the lease.**

The pet owner must take all responsibility for damage that was caused by the pet. This can be signed after a tenancy begins, but unfortunately you cannot force the tenant to sign it.

3. **Be vigilant about the property inspection.**

   While you must always complete a move-in inspection with photos and checklists and have the tenant sign off, it becomes extra important when pets are involved.

4. **If one tenant in a multi-unit building has an allergy, don't accept a pet in another unit.**

   Never state the pet as the reason for not accepting a tenant. This opens you up for a human rights complaint.

5. **Don't accept large dogs in a carpeted property.**

   Large dogs tend to ruin carpets and are better suited to properties with hardwood floors and laminate floors.

Policy on Illegal Activities

Tenants must be firmly warned against illegal activities of any kind. The following are the three steps to take regarding illegal activities:

1. **Let tenants know that you have a zero tolerance policy for illegal activities.**

   When illegal activities take place on the premises, it's affecting your reasonable enjoyment of the property as a landlord. This gives you legal ground to end the tenancy.

2. **Call police immediately.**

3. **Issue an N6 to evict immediately.**

   Make sure you document the entire process carefully.

The challenge with this process is that the illegal act must be serious enough to disturb the character of the premises or the reasonable enjoyment of the landlord or other tenants. It can't be something like writing a bad cheque, but needs to be something very serious like selling drugs.

Policy on Maintenance

Maintenance is a big part of your job as a landlord. It's not that you'll do the maintenance yourself (although you may do some of it), but you'll have to coordinate all of the maintenance of a property. This job multiplies with multiple properties.

If you haven't experienced it yet, you'll have to believe me that it can be a *huge* job. I would say it's one of the main reasons for landlords burning out and exiting the investment real estate realm.

But this is only a problem if it's not done correctly. By implementing solid policies and following them to a T, effective landlords will find themselves ahead of maintenance issues rather than one step behind, which is where so many landlords end up. The following policies are designed to streamline the landlord's maintenance processes:

1. **Group together as many maintenance and repairs as you can at the same time.**

   This could be a weekly or monthly schedule. Rather than having contractors go back to a property numerous times for small jobs, it makes more sense to take care of multiple issues on one visit.

2. **For each property, create a file that anticipates major repairs.**

This would relate to the major systems and structures and of the property: roof, HVAC, Hot Water Heater, foundation, major appliances. In addition, information on flooring and painting of the property should also be noted.

3. **For each property, create a maintenance plan that breaks down necessary repairs into specific time frames.**

   This maintenance plan should be biweekly, monthly, quarterly, biannually and annually tasks. The maintenance plan on a multiunit building will have to be more intensive than a single-family home.

The major repairs and maintenance plans are vital to the streamlining of maintenance. These can be used to impress upon tenants that there is a plan in place, and that you'll take care of repairs in due course. In addition, the plans allow you to make financial budgets for any repair needed. Joint venture partners also like to see these plans, and you will impress bankers with your level of preparation by sharing them. It's worth going over the process of creating these plans here. Below is a rundown of the process for creating and organizing the major repair and maintenance plans:

1. **Keep maintenance request forms in the tenant's binder at the property.**

   Explain to tenants that this form is required to be completed for any maintenance to be done. Once the form is received, you can integrate it into your maintenance plan and communicate the timeline for maintenance with the tenant.

2. **Keep a plastic portfolio with 4 separate folders.**

This is like a small moveable filing cabinet. It looks like a binder and has attached elastic to keep the flap closed.

The four folders will contain a) Maintenance Inspection Reports, b) Tenant Information (including maintenance request forms), c) Upcoming Repairs (based on maintenance inspection reports and tenant maintenance requests) d) Quarterly and Year-End Co-Venture Reports.

3. **Use combined information from the portfolio to create a maintenance and major repair plan.**

This level of organization, planning, communication, and tracking is required in order to ensure that maintenance is done efficiently and within budget.

Tools Found in A Landlord's Basement

You might be thinking tools like hammers, wrenches, a socket set, or screwdrivers, but there are a few other tools that I recommend every landlord purchase and store just in case of an emergency. You may never need or want any of these tools, or you might go directly to a service provider, so think about each item and what you personally would do in case of an emergency.

Backup Heaters/Blankets – If the furnace goes out in one of your properties in the middle of the winter, you should have backup heaters and a stack of blankets ready to go. I have backup oil-based radiator units that run on electricity. They can heat about 500 square feet of open area, enough to keep the temperature above zero in a property where the heat has gone. Not only will your tenants appreciate it, but you could also be stopping the pipes from freezing.

Backup Ceramic Stove/Toaster Oven – If the stove in your property has failed and it may take a few days before you can the stove replaced, it is a good idea to provide this inexpensive alternative to tenants.

Small Gas Generator – In case the power goes out and you need to power those backup heaters, a small gas generator will allow them to function. These generators have come down significantly in price, and I have seen solid generators sold for less than $400.

Water Jet Pump – These little pumps can help you quickly move water out of a property, in case of an emergency. There are many different types of pumps, but I would suggest a small pump that can support the movement of water through a garden hose.

Industrial Fan – These powerful fans are great for quickly drying wet carpets or areas where work has been done or you have had water come into a property. Get a size that suits the type of properties that you own.

Ozone Generator Machine – These handy tools have come down in price, so that now even small-scale landlords can afford to purchase them. You need to follow the directions carefully and make sure the property is vacant when used, but they do a great job in eliminating smells from a property. Ozone generators create O3, or ozone, which helps to remove stubborn odours from a property—think pet or cooking smells.

Policy for Balconies

1. **Balconies and patios are not to be used for drying clothing or storage.**

   The balcony and patio area forms part of the aesthetic appeal of the property. Just as it's the tenants' responsibility to maintain the cleanliness of other parts of the property, they must also keep the balcony and patio tidy.

2. **Tenants are not to clean mops, brooms, or dust carpets on the balconies.**

Policy on Guests

A landlord can't typically limit guests at a property. It's a tenant's right to have guests in their home just as a homeowner does. But it *is* in the landlord's interest to monitor guests.

Hopefully, with excellent tenant screening, you won't end up with a party house. This is a nightmare scenario for landlords. The assorted relaxed and in-control gathering of friends shouldn't concern you too much.

What can be concerning is a 'guest' you find is suddenly at the property all the time. This often happens when a tenant gets a new boyfriend or girlfriend. When you find there's a new person suddenly at the property on a regular basis, it's wise to find out as much about them as you can.

Consider some of the consequences. What if there was a medical emergency on the property. Who would you inform if the 'guest' became ill or injured? What if the 'guest' was in conflict with one of the other tenants in a multi-unit building? What can you do about a non-tenant causing problems?

If you find there's a new guest spending a lot of time on the property, you must be proactive about it. Follow these policies for guests in one of your rental properties:

1. **Explain to tenants that the number of guests in a property is governed by local bylaws and health and safety standards**. For example, the City of Cambridge Building and Property Standards By-Law (http://www.cambridge.ca/byLaws/04-181%20Building%20&%20Property%20Standards%20By-law.pdf) states that the "The maximum number of occupants in a dwelling unit shall be based upon two persons per bedroom."

2. **Ask tenants for the names of any guests and a copy of the guests' driver's licenses.**

There's no way to enforce this, but it doesn't hurt to ask. Don't tell them they have to provide this by law, just tell them it's one of your requests so you can monitor activity.

3. **Communicate with tenant that they are responsible for their guests.**

This only usually becomes a problem when a guest in another suite complains.

4. **File an eviction of occupant immediately if you believe a new tenant has replaced an existing tenant either through assignment of the lease or by other means.**

The form to accomplish this is the A2 form. Do this immediately and get the unapproved tenant out if it should ever happen to you.

The law in Ontario states that landlords have 60 days to get a new tenant out of the property if they've replaced the original tenant. And if they're not out by that time, the landlord legally must assume the new tenant!

As you can imagine, this is a highly undesirable situation! If it's not a tenant that *you* selected, you don't want them living in your property. Period. Even if you meet them, get to know them, and they seem likeable, you don't want to keep a tenant who came into your property in this way.

If they found their way into your property without you knowing it, it's a good indication that something dodgy is going on. Get the new 'tenant' out before the 60 days is up, using the A2 form. Find a new tenant and move on. The consequence of not getting them out within 60 days is that you might end up battling to get them out for months. Once someone is legally your tenant, it's much harder to get him or her out than it is if you follow the procedure properly. File the A2 form immediately.

Policy on Keys, Locks and Lockboxes

Securing the property is of utmost importance. As with all aspects of the business, a successful landlord will seek to implement a system that maximizes efficiency, convenience, speed, and thrift. The following policies on keys, locks, and lockboxes are designed to achieve this:

1. **Use the Weiser Smart Lock system.**

   When a new tenant takes over, the locking mechanism must be changed. The Weiser Smart Lock system allows you to quickly change the locks on the property and use new keys.

   This system saves a great deal of time every time the property is newly tenanted. By inserting the old key, and then the Weiser Smart Key, and then the new key (and turning it halfway) the lock is immediately re-keyed. The whole process takes about 30 seconds, a big improvement over the traditional option of changing out the lockset.

   There are several reasons for employing this lock system is a good idea. First of all, there's the cost of replacing a lockset each time a new tenant moves out. Second, it takes *you* time to replace it, and it since you're not an expert, you may not do it properly. Third, the other option is hiring a locksmith, which carries additional cost and time spent coordinating with the locksmith.

   Do yourself a favour and follow this policy.

2. **A spare key for every property must be labeled on the keychain and held in a lockbox in the office.**

   Do this the same day you change the lock with the Weiser Smart Key.

3. **A lockbox with a spare key must be located on the property.**

The lockbox code should never be given to the tenant unless it's an emergency, like if you're out of town and the tenant requires a key because they've locked themselves out of the property.

Once the tenant has entered the property and located their original key, they must put the key back. Then you change the lockbox code at your earliest convenience.

Another time to use the key inside the lockbox might be when there is a vital or emergency repair that needs to be done to the property when both you and the tenant are unable to get to the property.

In this case, it's important to obtain the tenant's approval, and again it's important to change the lockbox code at your earliest convenience.

Policy on Rental Signs and Other Signs

1. **"For Rent" signs are to be placed in the upper windows of a property when it becomes available to rent.**

This may not be possible in condominium properties, depending on the condo bylaws. In addition, you may only do this if your tenant approves it. I've never had a problem with a tenant approving it.

I find onsite signs to be one of the most effective methods of advertising a property for rent because it attracts people who are already in the neighbourhood. Perhaps they work nearby or perhaps they have family and friends in the area. Whatever the case, if they call, it means they're ready to live at that location. This means they only have to be sold on the property and the landlord. I find that potential tenants who call from a sign are generally more serious than some of the other people who call using other methods of advertising.

2. **Tenants may not display signs for personal businesses on the property.**

The only business to be run on the property is your rental property business. It's not a good idea to let tenants operate any sort of business on the property.

Policy on Waterbeds and Aquariums

1. **No aquariums, waterbeds, or similar devices are allowed at the property.**

Waterbeds and aquariums have been known to leak. On one occasion the entire contents of a waterbed leaked over the course of a weekend. The leak was slow enough that the tenant didn't notice it immediately, but eventually the basement tenant noticed. By then the bedroom ceiling drywall and one wall of the bedroom was completely destroyed.

The best policy is simply to state that large bodies of water are not to be stored in any device on the property other than the hot water tank.

The property rules in the lease should state that these large water volume devices aren't allowed, and that tenants will be held responsible for any damage caused by them.

Policy on Rental Applications, Leases and Other Forms

This is not an exhaustive list of items that can help prepare you to place a new tenant into a rental property, as I plan to go into more depth on this process in a future manual. But for now, here are a few things to consider.

1. **Do a credit check on each tenant before you approve.**

   As landlords in Ontario, we're severely limited in the measures we can take to learn about applicants for our properties. We can't perform a criminal record check, and there's no legal database of problem tenants.

   The credit check is one of the few methods we're allowed to check up on a potential tenant. One day this might also be taken away as a right, but in the meantime, it's necessary for landlords to learn as much about the tenant as they possibly can. Therefore, pull a credit report on each tenant. Learn how to read them and screen for the best tenant possible.

2. **Contact the tenant's second last landlord before approving.**

   Most landlords try to contact the tenant's most recent landlord before approving the tenant. I no longer bother calling the most recent landlord. I find this most recent landlord to be an unreliable source of information because they're still too attached to the outcome to give a sound account of the tenant's history.

   In some cases, the most recent landlord doesn't want to lose the tenant, so they'll give an intentionally bad review of the tenant's history. In other cases, they want to get rid of the tenant, so they give a poor review.

The second last landlord is sufficiently detached from the situation and can provide an honest appraisal of the situation.

3. **Keep secure digital copies of all consents for credit check, including completed rental applications.**

At this time, the proof of consent should be maintained for at least seven years by law.

4. **When consent to a credit check has been provided, only share the results with the person on whom the credit check was done and never with their partner or spouse.**

This is your legal obligation to keep that tenant's information private.

5. **If you deny an applicant, do not mention the credit check.**

Due to the nature of human rights laws, it's best to only say "I have decided to go with another tenant." This policy can be expanded to almost any situation. It's always best not to give a reason, since you can't be sure what reasons could be construed as a violation of human rights. Using a tenant's bad credit could be construed as a bias against a tenant based on their financial situation.

6. **Do not rent to friends or family unless you are willing to 100% break all ties with the person/family if the tenancy deteriorates.**

This is a business. There are several ways to help out family and friends without renting a property to them.

For the same reason I suggest you don't become buddies with tenants, I also suggest you don't rent to your existing buddies or family. There is an unspoken expectation that you'll give them a break since you know them.

To maintain the integrity of your business, it's best not to rent to family and friends. Because you likely don't want to cut off all ties with a family member or friend, it's best to simply not rent to them.

7. **Copies of all rental applications, leases, amendments, and separate agreements should be kept electronically as well as in the filing system.**

   Just as with electronic data, it's important to keep hard copies secure and well organized. It helps you avoid big problems in the future.

8. **Electronic copies of all forms that are submitted should be kept.**

   This adds another layer of redundancy to your system and is an excellent idea.

PROPERTY MANAGEMENT PROFILES
ANDREW BRENNAN: NEAR DEATH EVENT

A property manager or landlord should abide by the dictum: "Expect the unexpected." While you can't predict exactly what will happen, you can be sure of one thing – situations will arise. I'm not speaking of normal day-to-day problems; I'm talking about those rare scenarios that make you sit back and scratch your head, saying aloud, "Wow, I never saw that coming."

But excellent preparation ensures that you'll be prepared even in the event of some of the most unexpected circumstances. Take for example the rare circumstance veteran investor and property manager, Andrew Brennan, experienced a couple years back.

In every tenancy, Andrew goes through a close inspection with the tenants and has them sign off on a special section stating that the smoke detector and CO2 detector are working properly. The tenant has to sign that it's their responsibility to keep the detectors in working order. Andrew does this for every tenancy, and he did it again when two female university students moved into one of the suites in one of his duplex properties.

The students had moved in at the beginning of their first semester at the University and all was going well. They'd lived in the suite for not much longer than a month when Andrew received a call from one of the two students mentioning that something was wrong with the hot water heater at the property. It wasn't working properly, so Andrew immediately called *Direct Energy*, his natural gas provider for the property.

Direct Energy sent a technician to the property the next day to begin an investigation into the hot water heater problem. What the technician found while there was frightening. As it turned out, there was a collapsed liner inside the chimney. The collapsed liner was blocking the furnace exhaust gas from escaping. The CO_2 from the exhaust gas was building up in the chimney and pushing back into the house, causing a dangerous buildup of deadly CO_2 in the property.

The technician implemented the emergency procedures and called in the gas leak investigation team. What they found was a series of events that nearly led to the tenants' death—and to their ultimate survival.

First, the liner had collapsed, which is rare. In Andrew's time as a landlord, he'd never seen or heard of another case of a collapsed chimney liner. Second, the tenants alerted Andrew to an unrelated problem, the faulty hot water heater. Third, the CO_2 detector, which had recently been inspected and was working, was found to have a battery placed backwards in it. The tenants had replaced the battery and had not thought to double check that the battery was properly installed or to test that the detector was working. If the detector had been installed properly, the tenants would have been alerted by a loud alarm. Fourth, the weather that October was unseasonably warm, which meant that the furnace had barely been turned on at all. The inspection team surmised after the fact that if the weather had been just a bit cooler, the tenants would have died from CO poisoning. As it was, the air was just barely safe to breathe when the inspectors took tests. Only one or two more cold evenings could have been enough to kill the tenants.

Luckily for Andrew, he'd taken every precaution possible to avoid such a dangerous situation, and he acted quickly to remedy the problem of the faulty hot water heater. No landlord wants tenants to die in his unit, especially from a preventable accident.

The lesson here is simple. Unknown circumstances can arise without warning, and sometimes they can be serious. As a landlord, you have other people's lives in your hand, indirectly, if not directly. For the sake of your own conscience and liability, it's more than crucial that you take every precaution to avoid putting yourself in a compromising situation.

If things had gone the other way and the tenants had passed away from that series of unfortunate events, Andrew would have at least been secure in the knowledge that he'd done everything necessary to avoid the problem. Part of successful landlording is covering yourself so that you can sleep at night.

This means being properly insured, but it also means taking physical and legal precautions. Acting quickly in a serious situation is also vital. Think about how much worse Andrew's situation could have been without his painstaking preparation and precaution.

To be successful as a landlord, please emulate Andrew. Take the time to think through possible outcomes, and take the necessary precautions to allow yourself (and your tenants) to sleep at night.

Policy on Renovations and Repairs

Renovations and repairs will form one of the biggest aspects of your job as a landlord, and they will be one of the biggest sources of non-recurring expense and capital expenditure. These policies are designed to streamline the renovations and repairs process:

1. **Use the Weiser Smart Key and lock system for door locks.**

   See above policies on locks for further explanation.

2. **Contact the local building supply store and ask if you can access a contractor card or a discount card based on your real estate business.**

   The discount and benefits you're able to secure with these contractor cards varies depending upon the store and how much you spend.

   Search all of the big box store and building supply stores to find out what bonuses work best for you.

3. **Use the same paint color in all properties.**

   This makes it easy when there's a patch job. Rather than having to paint an entire room or wall, and rather than having to seek out unique color, you will just know it's the same color you always use.

   It's also handy when purchasing paint because you can do so in bulk. By searching for deals and then buying in bulk, you can save thousands on paint, but this only works if every property has the same color.

   I like to use a mushroom brown color CIL brand base 81,200 premium eggshell low luster paint for all interior jobs.

   For doors and trim, I use CIL's standard white trim and door paint, a semi-gloss product.

4. **Use the same light and plumbing fixtures in each property.**

   This makes repairs easier. I use Moen faucets because I can call the company up and get replacement parts at no charge.

   Just as with the Weiser Smart Key system and using standard paint colors, this policy helps simplify your process. As with paint, you can seek deals and buy these products in bulk so you always have an inventory of fixtures available.

One caveat on this policy is to not replace properly working faucets and light fixtures just to get them the same as the rest of your system. Wait until the needs arises, maximizing your maintenance renovations expenditures.

5. **The more building products that can be used the same way in similar properties, the easier it will be to manage the repairs.**

Apply the same principle across all standardly used parts. Paint, locks, light fixtures, and faucets are the most common examples, but perhaps you can find other commonly used parts to apply the rule of uniformity to.

6. **When possible, install low flush toilets.**

This is a solid renovation for marketing and systematizing. You'll be seeking to put the onus of utilities on your tenants, so cost of water usage won't be a problem. However, it's a good idea to show tenants you care about their expenses.

As with faucets, don't replace the toilet until it's needed.

7. **On jobs above $1000 (siding, roof, windows), get at least three quotes from independent contractors.**

There is often significant variance on price and delivery on these bigger jobs; therefore, it's important to seek out the best price. Getting only one quote can be very costly.

8. **When a unit becomes vacant, take the opportunity to upgrade the property to justify higher rents.**

This is one of those aspects of landlording that is more art than science. It's extremely difficult to judge how much more rent you can justify on a property on which you've done renovations.

9. **Renovate for cosmetic appearance.**

Hopefully, you inspected the property for structural issues when you purchased it (or did major renovations at the time of purchase). Remember, you bought the property for a reason.

The main renovations required should be ongoing small improvements to the most worn out parts of the property. Major capital expenditures are to be treated differently and planned for accordingly.

10. **Focus on renovations that will provide the biggest rental increase.**

Whenever you put money into the property, you want the property to be able to pay you back relatively fast. The best rule of thumb is to recapture the expense of the renovations within 2 years.

This isn't an exact science, but if, for example, you spend $2500 renovating a property, you should be able to raise the rent about $105 per month, which works out to just over $2500 over 24 months (2 years).

11. **Do market research to develop your upgrade plan.**

Take a look at the homes on Kijiji and Craigslist to see what the rental competition is like. Take note of what you see in the pictures. Based on the condition of comparable rental properties, you can make decisions with regards to upgrades without over-renovating. Always keep in mind the tenant profile of your property whenever you are doing any upgrade (translation: no granite countertops for a working class rental unit!).

Focus on the following renovations to achieve maximum results:

Kitchen

1. Clean appliances or replace. Upgrade any old yellow or green appliances.

2. Add a backsplash with a tile inlay

3. Replace cabinet handles

4. Replace faucet

5. Replace light fixtures

6. Replace countertop

7. Replace flooring

8. If necessary, re-stain cabinets or reface/replace

Bathroom

1. Clean fan

2. Replace faucet

3. Replace light fixtures

4. Replace sink

5. Replace countertop and/or mirror

6. If necessary, re-stain cabinets or reface/replace

7. Replace and upgrade flooring

8. Replace toilet

9. Re-spray tub or replace

Curb Appeal

1. Remove any garbage

2. Sod and seed yard as necessary

3. Prune existing trees and shrubs

4. Plant new perennial shrubs (low maintenance plants only)

Across Entire Property

1. Paint entire house and repair walls

2. Clean carpets

3. Replace carpets and/or upgrade to laminate

4. Change light fixtures

5. Change switch and plug plates to white

Maintenance Plans

Each property should have a maintenance plan that breaks down the necessary maintenance needed at that particular property. These tasks increase when the property is vacant.

1. Each plan must be customized to the property.

Generic maintenance plans don't work because each property will have its own specific needs.

2. **Each plan must be broken into different phases of the year: bi-weekly, monthly, quarterly, bi-annually, and annually.**

See sample plans below:

Single Family or Duplex Maintenance Plan

Quarterly:

1. Review possible capital expenses for the property.

2. Do a drive-by inspection of the property.

Bi-Annually:

1. Ensure smoke alarms and CO alarms are all working – complete CO/smoke alarm test.

2. Complete spring or fall bi-annual inspection and inspection report.

3. Ensure furnace filters have been changed.

4. Ensure outside water has been turned off for the winter or turned on for the spring.

5. Service furnace/air-conditioner/water heater as necessary.

6. Caulk around bathtubs, sinks, and countertops as necessary.

7. Make note of capital expense items that will need to be replaced due to wear and tear in the near future.

Multi-Family Maintenance Plan

Biweekly:

1. Ensure stairways and foyers are clear.

2. Check property common areas for burned-out light bulbs or graffiti.

3. Make sure lawn is cut, leaves are raked, and snow is cleared.

Monthly

1. Ensure that the laundry facilities are cleaned and in good working order.

2. Collect any money from machines.

3. Ensure that crawl spaces are free from the debris.

4. Ensure that parking lot and trash bins are clear.

Quarterly

1. Examine the common areas for wear and damage.

2. Ensure boilers, furnaces, and air conditioners are working appropriately.

3. Ensure common area doors and locks are working appropriately.

Bi-Annually

1. See if the window exteriors require cleaning.

2. Ensure that bushes and trees are trimmed.

3. Ensure gardens and plants are being taken care of.

4. Inspect the roof, gutters, foundation, siding, and parking lot to be sure that they are clean and in good shape.

Annually

1. Ensure boiler, furnace, air conditioning, and water heaters are inspected.

2. Ensure smoke alarms and CO2 alarms are all working.

3. Clean carpets in the common area and on the stairs.

Vacant Property Maintenance Plan

Please keep in mind that the insurance policy may allow for a 60-day vacancy, but there may be the opportunity to extend coverage beyond 60 days. Make sure to communicate to the insurance company during the vacancy. The insurance company may also require that you visit the property every few days to ensure that there are no issues; inquire about the number of days because it differs depending on the insurance company. Most insurance policies will want you to comply with the following conditions:

Weekly (Depending Upon Your Insurance)

1. Check that all doors and windows are securely closed and locked.

2. Remove rubbish from buildings and premises.

3. Shut off water supply and the system and drain all appliances.

4. Maintain heat in the building.

5. In addition, a vacant property offers the opportunity for property improvement. See above guidelines for improving vacant properties.

Inspections

Regular inspections are a vital part of a landlord's job. They're vital for maintenance planning, maintaining strong relationships with tenants, and ensuring there's no illegal activity in your properties. Use the following policies for inspections:

1. Inspections should be carried out bi-annually and within the first three months of re-tenanting a property.

2. Whenever a general inspection for defects takes place, there must also be a fire and CO Inspection.

3. 24 hours' written notice in the proper format must be given to a tenant.

The exception to this rule is if you have a written response (letter or email) from a tenant permitting a maintenance request in a shorter time frame.

4. Contact the tenant by email and let them know you will be doing a fire and CO alarm check.

Mention at the same time that you'll be addressing any maintenance issues.

5. Give full 24 hours' notice of inspection and hand deliver if tenant doesn't approve the maintenance request by letter or email or if the tenant is belligerent.

This can be put between the screen door and door, handed to the tenant, or slipped under the door. If it's put between the screen door or slipped under the door. take a picture of the notice and make note of the date and time. Sample note below:

NOTICE OF ENTRY FOR INSPECTION

Date: June 28th, 20XX
Mr. Thomas Tenant, 222 Maple Street
Whitby, Ontario, B2B 2B2

Dear Mr. Tenant:

I will be entering your rental unit on June 30th, 20XX, at or shortly after 11 am. I will remain in the rental unit for approximately 2 hours.

The purpose is so that I may perform fire alarm, CO_2, and maintenance inspections.

You are not required to be there at the time of entry, as I don't wish to inconvenience you. But, if you are not planning on being in attendance, you must make sure there are no devices blocking entry such as chain locks. You must ensure that any animals are tied up or are not in the unit. Also, please disarm any alarms that might interfere with entrance into the unit.

Thanks for your patience; I do apologize for any inconvenience this may cause.

I am giving you this notice in accordance with the Residential Tenancies Act. If you attempt to impede entry, I will contact the Ministry of Municipal Affairs and Housing's Investigations and Enforcement Branch and ask them to lay charges. An offence under the Residential Tenancies Act carries with it a fine up to $25,000 upon conviction. Please feel free to call the Investigations and Enforcement office at 416-585-7214 to learn about your obligations with respect to entry.

Sincerely,

Name Of landlord

Fire and CO2 Inspections

Once you've gotten into the property following the correct means, your next job is to actually perform the inspections. Follow this procedure for fire and CO2 inspections:

1. **Fire and CO2 Inspections are done at the same time as the regular inspection.**

2. **Ensure smoke and CO2 detectors are in good working order.**

3. **Make sure all fire doors close properly.**

4. **Inspect for overloaded circuits.**

5. **Look for garbage around the furnace/boiler room.**

6. **Make sure fire doors are accessible and fire rated.**

7. **Include a fire extinguisher in the kitchen.**

8. **Include instructions on how to operate smoke detectors.**

9. **Clean out dryer vents annually.**

10. **Use the fire/CO2 Inspection Form.**

    Complete a copy of this report either a) in duplicate immediately or b) scan and email a copy to the tenant. File this inspection form with associated documentation for the property.

11. **Include 'in case of fire' instruction notices on the back of each front door of property.**

    See sample instruction below:

ATTN: RESIDENTS OF NAME OF PROPERTY

Fire Procedures:

1. Leave the fire area.
2. Close all doors behind you.
3. Alert all other building occupants if safe to do so by knocking on suite doors and yelling "Fire!"
4. Exit the building and call Whitby Fire and Emergency Services by dialing 911 —never assume this has been done. Know the correct address of the property.
5. Do not return until it is declared safe to do so by the fire department officials.

If you live in a suite and are alerted of a fire:

1. Exit your home. NEVER EXIT INTO THE GARAGE.
2. Follow instructions given by the Whitby Fire and Emergency Services.
3. Do not return to your home until authorized by fire department officials.

If you're in a garage and discover a fire:

1. Leave the fire area.
2. Close all doors behind you.
3. Activate the fire alarm, if accessible.
4. From a safe place, telephone Whitby Fire and Emergency Services at 911 —never assume this has been done.
5. Give the correct address of the building.
6. Do not return until authorized by fire department officials.

If you're in the underground parking facility and hear a fire alarm:

1. Leave the area using the nearest stairwell.
2. If you encounter smoke in the stairwell, consider taking an alternative exit where it may be clear.
3. Do not return until it is declared safe by the fire department.

HVAC Inspection

The HVAC system in your property is one of the most expensive to replace. Therefore, it's one of the most important to inspect and maintain. Follow these policies for HVAC inspections:

1. **Perform HVAC inspections once a year.**

   Use only qualified HVAC technicians for the inspection.

2. **Label furnace filters by month and have tenants replace them.**

   If this is not possible, then make sure the filters are cleaned at least twice yearly on the date of the maintenance inspection.

3. **Change the batteries in your thermostat yearly.** This is an easy way to avoid an unnecessary call to an HVAC technician.

Maintenance Inspections

Your maintenance inspections will form the basis of your maintenance plan, which is vital to increasing cash flow and making your life better as a landlord. Follow this set of proven policies for maintenance inspections:

1. Answer the following questions to inform your maintenance planning:

   a. When will the roof need to be replaced?

   b. When will the furnace, AC, or hot water heater need to be replaced?

   c. How is the building foundation?

   d. How long will appliances last? Are they under warranty?

e. Do the floors need to be refinished, carpets replaced?

f. Does the interior or exterior need painting?

2. Take pictures of all the shut-off values in each property. Label them with a tag that provides an explanation of what each thing does. Make sure your tenant knows where they are and how to use them.

Drive-By Inspections

As you'll recall, drive-by inspections are suggested quarterly for single-family homes and duplexes. Follow these policies for drive-by inspections:

1. **This inspection should note any tenant issues and any apparent maintenance issues visible from the outside of the property.**

2. **If possible get out and walk around the property.**

3. **Note any peeling paint, loose shutters and eaves trough problems.**

4. **Step back and visually inspect the roof for debris or shingles that might have come loose.**

5. **Inspect electrical lines, cable lines, and phone lines coming out of the facility, along with any satellite dishes mounted on the facility.**

   Call the appropriate repair people if any damage is identified.

6. **Ensure security devices are in working order if any exist.**

7. **Ensure downspouts are away from property.**

8. **Look for grading and drainage issues.**

9. **Check with neighbours about any property issues.**

10. **Inspect for signs of a grow op:**

    a. Look for windows that are never uncovered.

    b. Look for snow melted away around the house and on the roof.

    c. Look for extra exhaust vents.

    d. Check with local police about any activity.

    e. Check local hydro if there's ever been a bypass.

    f. Talk to the neighbours.

    g. You may need to carry out an air quality tests, which can cost $1000-$3000

    h. Check information and ask the tenants questions; if they're lying, it will show up.

    i. Make sure tenants understand that police will be notified of any illegal activity.

Contractors

The following policies will properly govern your dealings with contractors:

1. **Always have two contractors for each trade that would be ready to move forward in case of an emergency.**

   It's unreasonable to expect a single contractor to be able to move at your whim. While contractors are often accommodating, especially for excellent customers who pay their bills promptly, there are times when they won't be able to help you immediately.

2. **Ask other landlords and real estate investors for contractor references.**

   The best contractors often come with several excellent recommendations. Visit your local real estate investment association or landlord group in order to network and find new tradespeople.

3. **Discuss expectations with each contractor.**

   Nothing can be as damaging to a business relationship as a misalignment of expectations. It's important you discuss and clarify the following topics with your contractors:

   a. Their insurance and WSIB coverage

   b. How the contractor will be contacted

   c. How they will contact you with what needs to be done

   d. Payment method

   e. Privacy—it is important to inform your contractor not to discuss the repair or something they may have noticed that needs to be fixed with the tenants

   f. References—ask contractors for at least two

   g. How they handle emergency calls

Follow these procedures for:
- Plumber

- Electrician

- HVAC Technician

- Handyman/General Contractor

- Appliance Purchase and Repair

Common Areas

Common areas are often left uncleaned because neither tenant wants to clean up after the other. There are some simple policies you can follow to be sure this doesn't become a problem. As always, tenant education is vital:

1. Educate each tenant on their individual common area clean-up responsibilities.

2. Create a generic clean-up schedule that divides the responsibilities between each unit.

   The schedule is to be posted where all tenants can see it and stays with the property regardless of tenant turnover.

3. Leave a broom, dustpan, and any other supplies needed so tenants can clean up after themselves.

"A business has to be involving, it has to be fun,
and it has to exercise your creative instincts."

— Richard Branson

Chapter 10

INSURANCE, LEASES, AND TENANCY ISSUES

Insurance on Rental Properties

In her excellent book, *Spend Smarter, Save Bigger,* Margot Bai gives a wonderful treatment of personal finance. In particular, I appreciate her discussion of insurance. I recommend everyone read the book.

The main point to realize about insurance is that you purchase it with the potential for a truly big and crippling expense. Insurance is purchased for the comfort of knowing that you can continue in your business if an expensive calamity was to happen.

An unexpected $30,000 or $40,000 expense is crippling to most people. Insurance allows you to survive such an expense and continue on your path to building wealth.

Small expenses, even ones caused by tenants or natural disasters, aren't what insurance is designed for. For one thing, the insurance deductible is often a similar cost as the expense itself.

Second, making a bunch of small claims will force the insurance company to raise your premiums, making insurance too costly. Third, insurance companies are often not flexible and responsive enough to bother dealing with for small claims.

As your portfolio of real estate investments grows, so will the chances that you'll eventually need insurance for a large claim. The following policies are provided to make sure you're well-insured to avoid a costly catastrophe:

1. **Don't take out an insurance policy without considering the following:**

   a. Tenant vandalism – To my knowledge, only Park Insurance, Hub Insurance, and State Farm will cover for this. If you approach the local insurance dealer you use for your cars and personal residence, there's a good chance they won't know what you're talking about.

   b. Extended Vacancy Clause up to 120 days – Many insurers won't cover a vacant property! It's imperative that you understand your policy regarding vacant properties. In some cases, you're required to visit the property every 3-5 days. There are specific rules around how the property must be heated as well. As the landlord, you must know and understand *all* your policy's rules pertaining to an empty property.

   c. Commercial General Liability to $2 million – Some recommend $1 million, but I don't feel comfortable without double that.

   d. By-laws coverage – If there's ever a disaster that causes serious damage resulting in drywall being taken off the wall, you may be forced to upgrade the electrical, HVAC, or plumbing to reflect the current building code.

The general rule is electrical, HVAC, and plumbing can be left as is as long as it's sealed in the walls. The building code demands it be upgraded once the drywall is removed.

If you're stuck in this situation, you'll want to be sure your insurance covers you because the added expense of bringing everything to code will be high.

e. Business income/rents actual loss sustained – If there's a problem that will cause the property to be vacated for a long period of time, you need to be covered against a loss of income.

Regardless of any catastrophe, the bank will require its mortgage payment and the taxes must be paid. Without income from the property, this expense will likely be a major calamity in your life.

f. Sewer backup – This problem can be very costly, bringing a loss of rent *and* high renovation expenses. Not all insurance policies cover it. Check that yours does.

g. Stated asset co-insurance – This means that if you ever had to rebuild, but your stated asset value was lower than the real cost of rebuilding, the insurance will still cover you. It's like insurance that covers you if you understate the value of your asset.

h. Replacement cost – If your property burns to the ground, would you be able to rebuild the same asset with the coverage from your insurance policy?

2. **Keep insurance details on each property on a separate spreadsheet.**

   Be sure to include the necessary steps when a property is vacant, and how long a vacancy is covered by insurance. Include the name of your insurer, local representative, insurance policy number, coverage, deductible, and expiration date details. Keep an offsite version of this spreadsheet. These steps guarantee that you always follow the insurers rules. Without following the rules closely, you're at serious risk of voiding the insurance policy.

3. **Make sure tenants know that their possessions are not covered by the property insurance you take out.**

   Your insurance serves the purpose of covering *you*. It's your job as a proactive landlord to be sure that your tenants understand this. To educate tenants, spend a bit of time speaking to them about tenant insurance, and take the additional step of ordering the brochure titled "Tenant's Insurance – Is it right for you?" from the insurance bureau of Canada and include it in the Tenant Binder. The cost has been free in the past. You may order it from this website: http://www.ibc.ca/en/Need_More_Info/Home_Insurance_Publications.asp

   Order these brochures in bulk so you will always have some on hand when a tenant binder requires one.

> Nobody wants to need insurance, but when the time comes when it *is* needed, you'll never have a more grateful moment than the moment you realize you *are* covered against a major calamity.

I've experienced one such occasion in my time as a landlord. It happened on a property that I was selling. In fact, we already had a signed contract to sell the property, and it was 3 days before closing when my realtor called me and said, "There's one and a half feet of water in the finished basement; you need to get over here immediately."

It turned out that the sump pump had stopped working approximately three days earlier, and the property started filling with water immediately.

By the time we caught the issue, $30,000 worth of damage had already been done. We had to undergo mold remediation, replace the basement drywall, replace the flooring, replace the hot water heater, and replace the HVAC system.

Initially, my insurer wasn't going to cover the damage, but luckily I was able to prove that I'd been at the property five days earlier by showing the notes I'd made during that visit. That particular insurance company's rule was that vacant properties must be visited every 5 days, so I barely managed to avoid the catastrophe of paying $30,000 out of pocket, which would have been a crippling expense for me.

In other cases, I've heard of tenants causing major damage. It's truly awful when a tenant willingly causes damage. Dirty tenants will often cause small damage in the range of $500-$1000, but this isn't for insurance to cover.

In one particularly terrible case, a fellow landlord told me about a tenant who put concrete in the drains and toilet. The tenant then left the house and let the water run. Needless to say, the entire house flooded and there was immense damage done.

In another case, I spoke to a landlord whose tenant had several dogs that urinated and defecated throughout the entire house. To try and hide the damage done by the dogs, the tenant pushed all of the feces into the vents of the house, causing an unbearable stink and forcing the landlord to replace all the ducting.

In both of these cases, the only thing that saved the landlord was a tenant damage clause included in their insurance. To my knowledge, there are only a few insurers in Canada that will cover against tenant damage. It's imperative that as a proactive landlord, you ensure you're covered against such an outcome.

Checklist for Insurance During a Vacancy

The period of time during an extended vacancy is a particularly important time for your insurance. Always know the *exact* rules of your insurance policy. This checklist is a solid guideline, but it's not replacement for following the specific rules of your policy:

1. Ensure that the building is checked every 5 days and that a log is kept of each visit.

2. Ensure that building will continue to be heated

3. Shut off the main water supply and drain all appliances of water

4. Ensure all doors and windows are secured.

5. Remove any garbage or rubbish from premises.

6. Inform insurance company when vacancy begins and when it has ended. Discuss when a coverage extension may be necessary.

New Property Checklist

Follow these policies immediately upon adding a new property to your portfolio:

1. **Setup new bank accounts for each new property and get cheques associated with this account.**

2. **Verify insurance has been set up with pre-approved payment, or that payment has been made for the year ahead.**

3. **Set up a folder for each property using the filing system.**

4. **Set up a bookkeeping template for the new property.**

5. **Develop a maintenance plan that includes biweekly, monthly, quarterly, bi-annually or annual tasks for each property.**

New Tenant Checklist

As a proactive and successful landlord, it's important that you treat tenants with the utmost respect. The following policies are designed to help you show your tenants that they're valuable clients from the beginning of the relationship:

1. **Have a welcome gift waiting for the tenant.**

   For example, you might consider leaving a seasonal indoor or outdoor plant.

2. **Leave a thank you note in clear sight for residents when they move in.**

3. **Visit within the first week of the lease.**

   You can answer any questions that they have about the house or appliances during that visit. The information given in pre-visits can be overwhelming. Giving tenants a chance to settle in and use the house, they will no doubt have a few questions.

4. **After the first six months, contact your tenant and ask what they like best about the home.**

   Also ask if there's one thing that needs to be taken care of. This shows a level of proactivity that tenants are probably not accustomed to.

5. **Send cards to tenants during holiday seasons.**

Storage Unit and Parking Spaces

Renting garages and other storage units on a property is an excellent way to improve cash flow. I recommend landlords do this if possible, however it's important to note a few unique things about this strategy:

1. **Leases for storage units and parking spaces do not fall under the Residential Tenancy Act.**

   You must have a lease for the term of the lease.

2. **Unlike a residential tenancy lease, this lease doesn't automatically renew in any way.**

3. **If a non-leaseholder accesses a parking space, leave a note on the person's car with a contact number.**

   In this letter, state politely that they're parking in a spot that doesn't belong to them.

   a. Contact the condo property manager to see if they have a policy regarding parking spots and storage units.

      Find out if they have a preferred towing company in the complex.

   b. Call a parking company to tow the car away.

4. **If a non-leaseholder accesses a storage unit, cut the lock on the storage unit and remove materials by leaving them outside the unit.**

Gifts

Giving timely gifts to tenants is an excellent way to show them you care and appreciate them being great tenants. I follow these guidelines for gifts:

1. **Christmas Gifts – A maximum $25 gift certificate for appropriate store (based on the tenant profile) is an acceptable Christmas gift.**

   This gift should be hand delivered with a shake of the hand and a wishing of Merry Christmas and Happy Holidays.

2. **Welcome Gifts – A maximum of $30 should be spent on a welcome gift.**

   A plant, nice bowl with fresh fruit, or a decorative vase has worked well in the past.

3. **Baby Gifts – If tenant is expecting a baby, be sure to send a card, at the very least.**

   I recommend getting a small gift basket worth a maximum of $30 to be spent on generic items that would work for both girls and boys.

Residential Tenancy Leases

There are several common scenarios that can arise with regard to the proper application of residential tenancy leases. Below, we'll discuss the correct process to deal with these situations.

1. **Once the tenant gives an indication that they'd like to end the tenancy:**

   a. Do a maintenance inspection of the property and keep note of all the issues present; compare them to when the tenant leaves the unit.

   b. Compare this with the move in inspection report and the move-in pictures of the property.

   c. Start your process for filling vacancies.

2. **If the tenant has verbally indicated they plan to end the lease, you must send the following letter:**

Date: April 20th, 20XX

Mr. Thomas Tenant, 222 Maple Street

Whitby, Ontario, B2B 2B2

Dear Mr. Tenant:

On April 18th 20XX you told me that you are intending to move out of your rental unit on June 30st, 20XX. You also wanted me to apply the last month's rent to May's rent.

Whenever notice is given it needs to:

- Be done in writing
- Identify the rental property
- Be signed

Indicates the date you intend to terminate the tenancy

Use a Landlord and Tenant Board approved form

Without these criteria, we are forced to take the position that notice has not been given. We cannot rely on a verbal conversation. We cannot apply your last month's rent deposit to May's rent as you have requested.

If you wish to properly formalize a notice to terminate your tenancy, please contact me and I will arrange for us to execute an N9 notice to terminate the tenancy. This notice complies with the Residential Tenancies Act and gives the proper 60 days' notice effective at the end of a rental period.

Sincerely,

Name of Landlord

3. **If the tenant gives less than 60 days' notice and has indicated that they plan to end the lease using an N9 but haven't provided proper notice, then send letter shown below.**

Please note: this applies whether the tenant is in a month-to-month lease or a 1-year lease.

Date: April 8th, 20XX
Mr. Thomas Tenant, 222 Maple Street
Whitby, Ontario, B2B 2B2

Dear Mr. Tenant:

I received your N9 notice of termination dated March 31th on April 6th. You informed me that you will be vacating the property and terminating the tenancy on May 27th, 20XX.

I do accept your notice to terminate the tenancy as proof that you intend to move out on that date you specified. However, your notice is missing some key information. You must provide the landlord with 60 days' notice, and it must be on the last day of the lease term or of the rental period.

Please take note of the following, if a notice is not given in accordance with The Residential Tenancies Act.

Arrears of rent when tenant abandons or vacates without notice:

88. (1) If a tenant abandons or vacates a rental unit without giving notice of termination in accordance with this Act and no agreement to terminate has been made or the landlord has not given notice to terminate the tenancy, a determination of the amount of arrears of rent owing by the tenant shall be made in accordance with the following rules:

1. If the tenant vacated the rental unit after giving notice that was not in accordance with this Act, arrears of rent are owing for the period that ends on the earliest termination date that could have been specified in the notice, had the notice been given in accordance with section 47, 96 or 145, as the case may be.

I do accept your notice, however your rent is still owed until the earliest date that it could have been specified, had the notice been properly given to me. You are obligated to pay rent until June 30th. 20XX, and we will be applying the last month's rent deposit to the month of June rent.

Your April and May rent will continue to be owed as it has in the past.

Sincerely,

Name of Landlord

Tenant Wants to End Tenancy
Before Lease Has Begun

Although the tenant might think there are no obligations in this case because he hasn't moved in, he does have contractual obligations upon signing the lease. It's very important to collect the first and last months' rent immediately upon lease signing. This allows you some leverage if this scenario should ever arise. Follow these policies in this situation:

1. **Make every effort to re-rent the property right away.**

2. **Withhold the first and last month's rent until a new tenant is found.**

3. **If a new tenant is found within 30 days, return the last month's rent but subtract any advertising costs related to finding the new tenant. Keep the first month's rent.**

   You must provide a receipt for these costs and prove it was a result of the tenant ending the tenancy before it began.

4. **If it takes the full 60 days to find a new tenant, don't return any of first and last month's rent.**

5. **Once a new tenancy is lined up, prepare the N11 – mutual agreement to end a tenancy – and have both the landlord and tenant sign it.**

Use the following letter for this scenario:

Date: June 28th, 20XX

Mr. Thomas Tenant, 222 Maple Street

Whitby, Ontario, B2B 2B2

Dear Mr. Tenant:

While we accept your notice that you don't intend to occupy the rental unit, we will recover the costs of filling this vacancy in accordance with the Residential Tenancies Act.

You have given us $3000 for first and last month's rent as indicated in the Rental Application. We are actively seeking a new tenant for the rental unit.

If we're able to find a new tenant whose tenancy agreement would begin earlier than 60 days of when your agreement should have begun, we will deduct advertising expenses and return those funds.

The Residential Tenancies Act states the following if notice is not given in accordance with the Act:

Arrears of rent when tenant abandons or vacates without notice

88. (1) If a tenant abandons or vacates a rental unit without giving notice of termination in accordance with this Act and no agreement to terminate has been made or the landlord has not given notice to terminate the tenancy, a determination of the amount of arrears of rent owing by the tenant shall be made in accordance with the following rules:

1. If the tenant vacated the rental unit after giving notice that was not in accordance with this Act, arrears of rent are owing for the period that ends on the earliest termination date that could have been specified in the notice, had the notice been given in accordance with section 47, 96 or 145, as the case may be.

If you have any questions about your obligation for giving notice and ending a tenancy, please contact the rental office and we will answer any questions you may have

Sincerely,

Name of Landlord

Tenancy Agreement Term Ends

One common fallacy that many landlords believe is that every tenancy must begin with a one-year lease. This is in fact false. A tenancy can start with a month-to-month lease just as easily as it can with a one-year lease.

1. **In most cases, tenancy agreements should move to month-to-month leases at the end of the first year.**

   If a tenant requests to have another year lease, do not immediately fill this request. It's a more flexible position to be in a month-to-month lease, especially when there is a low vacancy rate, so it's best to delay a tenant request for another one-year lease.

   A month-to-month lease allows you to get a tenant out more easily. As well, it allows you to raise rent at a different month than when the lease began. And if you should need to move into the property yourself or sell it, you may do so much easier and quicker if the tenant is on a month-to-month lease.

2. **If the property is a single family home, a duplex, or an area with a high vacancy rate, you may prefer a one-year lease as turnover is much more costly for these types of properties than with a multi-family.**

3. **For multi-family properties use, month-to-month leases**.

   This is because a month-to-month lease allows the landlord more flexibility to evict the tenant for reasons other than non-payment of rent.

4. In certain situations, you may want to have a tenant on another one-year lease.

This could be a situation for a property which is difficult to fill with a quality tenant, or perhaps you want the lease to end in the spring or early fall when there is higher demand for rental properties.

Date: June 28th, 20XX
Mr. Thomas Tenant, 222 Maple Street
Whitby, Ontario, B2B 2B2

Dear Mr. Tenant:

I hope you are enjoying the nice weather.

I wanted to inform you that the initial year term of the tenancy agreement will be expiring and that we'll be moving to a month-to-month term when the initial year term ends. All the other terms of the tenancy agreement will remain the same. If you'd like to end the tenancy at any time in the future, you'll need to provide 60 days written notice before the start of the rental period (first of the month).

As a convenience to you, we will also need new post-dated cheques for you, as I only have up until July 1st, 20XX. If you could mail me new post-dated cheques from August 1st, 20XX on, I would appreciate it. If you can't mail them, I can arrange a time to come by and pick them up. Just let me know.

Please make cheques payable to:

Name of Landlord

111 Oak Street, Whitby, Ontario, A1A 1A1.

The amount of monthly rent on the cheque should be $1500.

Sincerely,

Name of Landlord

Lease Sublets

Tenants have the right to sublet their property in Ontario. This rare situation requires some specific actions. Follow these policies:

1. You can't refuse an original tenant's sublet. Don't attempt to, or it could land you in trouble with the Landlord Tenant Board.

2. Ensure the original tenant understands that they're responsible for the property at all times.

   This means they'll be responsible for any damage caused by the subletting tenant.

Lease Assignments

This situation is trickier than a sublet. The tenant has the right to assign a lease, but the landlord has the right to refuse the assignment. However, if the landlord refuses the assignment, the tenant then has the right to end the lease with only a 30-day notice.

The 30-day notice doesn't have to be on a month end; therefore, it could leave the landlord with a mid-month or late-month vacancy. This exact situation happened to me. A tenant set their 30-day notice for June 3rd, which meant there was sure to be at least one month's vacancy while I tried to find a tenant.

Follow these policies if a tenant ever attempts to assign a lease.

1. **Don't accept the assignment unless you are absolutely comfortable with the new tenants and have done the proper due diligence.**

Would you give your customers the keys to the register? If not, why would you give your tenants the right to choose your next tenant? Once you allow the assignment of lease, the new leaseholder has all of the rights and responsibilities of the original tenant with one major difference: You didn't approve them.

As a landlord, you always want to ask for an N11, which is a mutual release of the existing lease. This is highly preferable for the landlord because it gives legal control of the property back to the landlord.

Once the N11 is signed, there's nothing the original tenant can do to change the process. If they do not move out, you can file an L3, which is an Application to Terminate a Tenancy – Tenant Gave Notice or Agreed to Terminate the Tenancy found on the Landlord and Tenant Board web site (http://www.ltb.gov.on.ca)

PROPERTY MANAGEMENT PROFILES
JEFF WOODS: INCARCERATED TENANT

Jeff Woods is an experienced Niagara Region investor and property manager. "We started out investing, but soon found we were great at fixing property management problems. People started calling us to fix their problems and we saw it as a perfect vehicle to supplement our investment business," said Jeff.

With over 100 units under management (split between his own and clients holdings), Jeff has seen many unique situations in his time as a property manager. Perhaps none of those situations was as unique as the time he had to visit a jail in order to get a former tenant to sign an N11 (mutual termination of lease).

"There was a situation where the tenant was accused of sexual assault. Obviously this was a terrible situation, and our number one priority was to secure access to the property and get it re-rented," said Jeff.

The property was a six-plex and the owner had done a poor job of property management, which led to the horrible situation of having some really bad tenants in the property, the worst of which (allegedly) committed one of the most despicable acts imaginable.

What's striking when speaking to Jeff—and most managers of large portfolios—is his businesslike treatment of serious problems. He even pointed out that the tenants were more than happy to gossip and complain about the incarcerated tenant, and perhaps they have every reason to want to do so, but Jeff unequivocally had a job to do in the bad situation, and that's what he did.

I couldn't agree more with Jeff's approach. One of the worst mistakes a landlord or property manager can make is to use too much emotion when trying to solve a problem. It's precisely the opposite quality that allows successful property managers and landlords to make correct decisions and execute upon their proper decision.

The landlord or property manager who engages with problems at the emotional level forgets his or her solemn duty. In some circles, this is known as the philosophy of 'git 'er done'. All kidding aside, this is the landlord's only job and guiding principle. Through effective relationship management, systems, and policies, the landlord or property manager seeks to avoid problems at all costs, but the arrival of *some* problems is inevitable, especially when the property manager (Jeff, in this case) thrives on solving the intractable problems of real estate investors.

The steps of Jeff's process were unique in the case of the incarcerated tenant. It wasn't as though Jeff had a ready-made handbook with easily laid out steps designed to remediate the problem he had at hand. The manual you're currently reading is designed to provide several of the policies and procedures that you'll need in day-to-day landlording. This manual will decode many of the concealed principles of excellent property management, but whenever a unique situation like the one Jeff was forced to deal with arises, it's vital that you're able to think on your feet.

These situations will happen. No manual can pretend to answer every question that might arise. For these totally unexpected situations, it's more important to have a theoretical understanding of the principles of effective property management.

In this example, Jeff knew the best solution to the problem before him was to seek a mutual release of the legally binding lease to which the landlord and the tenant had both agreed.

"I often say to people this business is called property management, but it should be called people management. The properties themselves are inert collections of steel, concrete, brick, and wood. They can't set fire to themselves, flood themselves, or punch holes in their own walls," said Jeff.

He makes a good point. With the rare exception of natural disasters (most of which can be protected against with preparation), it's the human element of property management that brings all of the challenges. Whenever a property manager deals with a tenant, a contractor, a neighbour, or anyone else having to do with the property, there exists the possibility for a problem or solution. Which one it is largely depends on the response of the property manager. I say 'largely' because there's always the possibility that it's the other party being the uncooperative one.

Even these rare uncooperative people, however, can often be managed effectively through excellent relational and communication skills. The incarcerated tenant had the potential to be such a problem relationship, but Jeff's commitment to the philosophy of 'git 'er done' and his clear and consistent communication with the former tenant led to a peaceful and effective solution.

As mentioned above, Jeff's actual process in this case had to be invented as he went along. There was no existing situation to be found in his or any other external policy manual. It was a matter of doing a little bit of detective work to locate the former prisoner turned inmate. Using clear thinking, Jeff and one of his staff property managers, Marcel, reasoned that the former tenant might be in the local remand center. It took only a few phone calls to figure out that, and indeed, the tenant was being held there.

Once they had located the former tenant, it took learning the remand center's process for making contact with the inmate. Marcel followed this procedure to make direct telephone contact, and it took little time to make arrangements to coordinate an in-person visit to the inmate.

Of course, Jeff and Marcel observed the normal communication- and relationship-building process. They sought to accommodate the former tenant so long as his requests were reasonable—and they did turn out to be. The only thing the tenant-become-inmate requested was that Jeff and Marcel remove certain valuable objects from this apartment and relocate them to one of his family members' homes.

Jeff and Marcel agreed to do this, and in return, the former tenant signed off on the N11, releasing Jeff's client from the lease with the incarcerated tenant. Notice that even in this unique circumstance, Jeff and Marcel realized that an effective relationship would be the best path to *solving the problem*. They relieved themselves of any external concerns, such as the accusations leveled at the inmate. Obviously the allegations against the tenant were very emotional, especially to thoughtful and caring people, but Jeff and Marcel didn't let the emotion of the problem affect their process.

I urge everyone reading this book to mimic Jeff and Marcel's actions in difficult situations such as this. Just 'git 'er done'; this will allow you to move your position forward day by day, as long as it is legal and ethical.

Tenant Requests Reference Letter

On occasion, a tenant will request a reference letter regarding their tenancy. Granting this request—if the tenant has been a good one—is a good idea as it helps maintain a strong relationship with the tenant. Here is a sample reference letter that I have given:

```
                                          Date: June 28th, 20XX

To Whom It May Concern,

This letter verifies that Thomas Tenant has been residing at a property
at which I'm landlord at 222 Maple Street, Whitby from to August 1st,
2012 to today.

Mr. Tenant has been an (excellent/good/decent) tenant.

His monthly payments are (always/normally) on time. Mr. Tenant has
also shown (excellent/good/decent) respect for the property.

If I can assist you with further information regarding this tenancy,
please feel free to contact me at 555-555-5555 or email@landlord.
com.


Sincerely,


Name of Landlord
```

Abandonment of Rental Property Not Related to Eviction

Follow these policies in case a tenant has abandoned the property
without being evicted:

1. **Be very careful to ensure the tenant has actually abandoned the unit.**

   If the tenant is not behind on their rent, then the property
   cannot be considered abandoned.

2. **If a tenant was issued an N4 and vacates the property on the termination date, then the property has been vacated and not abandoned.**

If this is the case, you'll need to follow the *Tenant has Vacated a Rental Property* process.

3. **Try to get information from the neighbours or other tenants.**

   Ask if they saw the tenant moving out, or if they saw a moving truck. Was another tenant told they were moving out? How about a neighbour?

4. **Find out if the utilities are switched off.**

   Did the tenant contact a utility company to switch utilities?

5. **Check to see if mail and papers have been collected?**

   If they're piling up, it's a good sign that the property has been abandoned. If they're not piling up, the tenant might not have abandoned the property yet.

6. **Keep log notes that indicate abandonment of the property in order to provide proof to the Landlord Tenant Board.**

   More often than not, the tenant is behind on rent, and this is an indication of abandonment. Here's a sample of log notes for a suspected property abandonment:

Date/Time	Log Notes
Jan. 23/12 4:30pm	I witnessed 1 weeks' worth of mail and papers from the mailbox and the front door. I looked in window and saw there's no furniture in the property.
Jan. 23/12 4:50pm	Jane Doe in Unit 2 witnessed tenant moving out. He had a moving truck and two guys helping.

7. **Give notice to the tenant and to the Landlord Tenant Board that the unit has been abandoned, and that you intend to dispose of the belongings.**

You can apply to the Landlord Tenant Board for an order to terminate the tenancy, but this process could take a long time. Giving notice of abandonment is a more efficient process, which is why I recommend it.

8. **Take date/time stamped pictures of any property that the tenant has left behind.**

9. **Give the following notice, addressed to their last known address – your rental property, to the tenant.**

Retain a copy of the notice to deliver to the landlord tenant board if the tenant shows up asking for belongings.

Date: June 28th, 20XX
Mr. Thomas Tenant, 222 Maple Street
Whitby, Ontario, B2B 2B2

Notice of Belief of Abandonment
Dear Mr. Tenant:
Regarding Address: 222 Maple Street, Whitby, Ontario
This notice is given pursuant to Section 79 of the Residential Tenancies Act, which states:
Abandonment of rental unit:
79. If a landlord believes that a tenant has abandoned a rental unit, the landlord may apply to the Board for an order terminating the tenancy. 2006, c. 17, s. 79.
The rent owed on this property is $1500

Any unsafe or unhygienic materials will be disposed of immediately. Any tenant belongings will be disposed of after 30 days. If you would like your belongings back, you will need to pay rent owed and moving and storage expenses for your belongings within 30 days.

If you have any questions please contact me at:

Name of Landlord
111 Oak Street, Whitby, Ontario, A1A 1A1

Sincerely,

Name of Landlord

10. **Wait 30 days after giving notice or obtaining an order from the Landlord Tenant Board to dispose of tenant belongings.**

Any "unsafe or unhygienic materials" can be disposed of right away.

11. **Don't wait 30 days to prepare property for re-rental.**

12. **Never give any belongings back to a tenant if rent is owed.**

The tenant must pay rent owed, storage costs, and moving costs before getting any belongings back.

Tenant has Vacated a Rental Property

Tenants may vacate a property when they've been issued a Notice of Termination and they comply with the notice by leaving the property.

Death of Sole Tenant in Rental Property

This is obviously a very unfortunate situation, but death will catch up with all of us one day. It inspired me to write this book. It is worth mentioning when considering what to do with a rental property. If it happens, or you suspect it has happened, in one of your units, follow these policies:

1. **Watch for signs.**

   When dealing with the death of the sole tenant in the property, there may be some outward signs that there is a problem. You might notice that the windows are full of flies or that there's a lot of junk mail piled up.

2. **Notify police immediately.**

3. **Don't touch anything.**

4. **If the body has been sitting for a while, you may need to hire a Trauma Scene Cleaning service. A couple of excellent resources are:**

   http://www.gtaclean.com   and   http://www. crimescenecleaners.ca

5. **Use the emergency contact information from the tenant applications to contact the right family or friends.**

6. **The tenancy is terminated 30 days after the death of the tenant.**

7. **You can't dispose of the tenant's belongings (except for unhygienic and unsafe materials) until 30 days after the tenant had passed away.**

   The estate or family members can claim the proceeds of the sale of tenant's contents (after deducting moving and storage costs) up to 6 months after the tenant's death.

PROPERTY MANAGEMENT PROFILES
CHRIS DAVIES: DEALING WITH DEATH

One of the scariest scenarios for any landlord or property manager is dealing with the death of a tenant. There is much to consider in such a circumstance and it's vital for effective landlords to deal with such a severe problem with a clear head. The landlord must exercise a great deal of caution at such a time and act as a leader for all parties involved.

Chris Davies is an Edmonton, Alberta based real estate investor and real estate agent with a long history in property management for someone only in his mid-30s. Chris grew up in a property management family: "My grandpa started the company in the late 80s, and before long my mom and dad had joined him in the full time property management business, which meant I started in the business from as soon as I was old enough to do work," says Chris.

From his early teenage years, Chris was involved in the property management business as an unlicensed assistant. "I did it all from painting fences to bookkeeping to hiring and firing contractors. I did everything in the business you can do without a property management or accounting license," says Chris.

By the time he was in his early 20s, he was being entrusted with some of the most serious tasks that a property management company does. It was on this backdrop of experience that Chris came to experience the death of a tenant for the first time.

The tenant was a 30-year-old man who'd always been prompt with his rent payments up until then. He lived in a one-bedroom apartment in a somewhat rough area of Edmonton, and Chris was already familiar with dealing with non-paying tenants in such buildings around the city. Still, this tenant had a good record of on-time payment, and when Chris spoke to the onsite manager, she informed him that the tenant's car was still in the parking lot, leading him to believe that something strange had happened.

"I told my dad that I was about to head down to the building to find out what was going on. My 'spidey senses' were tingling, and I said in passing, 'I bet he's dead'," says Chris. Owing to experience in such matters, Chris's dad responded, "Better call the police. Either way, it can't be a bad idea. If the tenant is alive, it means he owes us back rent, in which case the police presence will help convince him to pay up, and if he's dead or sick, it's best to be accompanied by the police when entering the suite."

Chris heeded his father's advice and immediately called the police. The drive from the city's west end to the downtown apartment building took approximately 20 minutes. In the time from when Chris headed to the property until he arrived, the police had already entered the suite and called the medical authorities.

"I parked my car and walked up to the building. There were flashing lights of the ambulance and police outside, and the suite door was open. I didn't try too hard to see the body, but one glimpse through the bedroom door was all it took to see the coroners placing the body into a body bag," said Chris.

Since the police had arrived ahead of Chris, they immediately began to follow their own protocol for suspicious situations. They found the onsite manager and asked her to open the door with her key. They let themselves in, found the lifeless body, and instantly called the medical authorities.

The situation was stressful for Chris, but was made much less so by his calling the police before going to the property. This is a brilliant example of a policy I want you to use in your own landlording or property management practice. *Always call the police before entering a property if you suspect a tenant may be deceased.* There are so many reasons for this. It protects you in so many ways. You want the authorities to be the ones to make first contact with a dead tenant. They will thoroughly investigate any death, and it's vital that you don't touch anything. If for some reason, you enter the property before the police, it's important not to touch anything which might lead to the scene being polluted.

The first thing that happens to a dead body is the muscles relax, causing all of the bodily fluids that were being held in by muscle contraction to leak out. This is a hazardous materials situation. In Chris's case, the tenant had committed suicide by pill ingestion and had been lying on the bed for days or weeks. The mess was significant.

It took a hazardous material cleanup crew to take care of the next step. "It wasn't like the cleanup crew had on level five biohazard cleanup gear or anything, but cleaning up after a tenant dies has to be treated like any natural disaster cleanup. You need a proper disaster cleanup crew to take care of the problem."

In a normal case of death in a suite, the dead tenant's family will inherit any money or belongings owned by the tenant, and all the post-death costs will be covered by the deceased's estate. In this case, the deceased had no family or possessions of any value. This meant that the tenant's burial had to be taken care of by the public trustee. Chris and his property management company were left to deal with the public trustee to attempt to recover the cost of the tenant's death (disposal of belongings, cleanup of suite, renovations). It turned out to be futile, as the public trustee doesn't cover any costs beyond burial of the deceased.

In the end, Chris accepted it as a learning experience. One thing had stood out to him, though. Something about the situation just hadn't felt right. It was that feeling that led him to mention his belief that the tenant was dead to his father, and it was his father's experience and intuition that led him to suggest calling the police in advance.

Chris's dad, Brent, had had a similarly intuitive experience a few years earlier. He made a routine visit to a tenant's property, but after asking around about the tenant he suddenly had the feeling that something wasn't right. After knocking and trying to find out if the tenant was in the property, Brent decided to open the door. This might have been a case of pushing the boundaries and entering a property without proper warning, but Brent had the feeling something was amiss. When he opened the door and saw the chain lock secured, he immediately knew something was wrong. He promptly returned to his car to retrieve the bolt cutters, and he let himself into the suite.

Once inside, he found the tenant lying on the couch having a stroke. He immediately called the ambulance, and the paramedics were able to save the man's life without serious damage being caused by the stroke. In a somewhat happy ending to the story, the man was returned home after the stroke and lived several more years. By following his intuition, Brent was able to save the man's life.

The more experienced you become as a landlord, the more you'll find that your intuition plays a role in these kinds of decisions. In any case, the landlord is well-advised to take the precaution that Chris took that day and call the police posthaste if you suspect the tenant is dead in the suite.

Re-Training Bad Tenants

Not every tenant is a great tenant, but you'll find that sometimes the tenant you feel is bad just needs to be retrained. This is often the case with an overly demanding tenant who seemingly has requests for work and repair every week. Other tenants consistently pay late or bounce cheques.

Here are the correct policies for dealing with bad tenants:

1. **Set boundaries about when and where a tenant can contact you other than an emergency.**

   Ensure that they understand what is deemed an emergency; let phone calls go to voicemail.

2. **If excessive repairs and maintenance are requested on the property, ask the tenant to pay for the repairs or let the tenant know that the repairs can be done with an increase in rent.**

   Take pictures of repairs if it is a repetitive repair. Obviously, you can't do this if the repairs are reasonable, but some tenants demand repairs that a landlord would never put on their maintenance plan because it's unimportant or unnecessary. An example would be a tenant requesting new windows put into a rental property or adding additional insulation to the attic.

3. **If a minor problem keeps recurring, teach the tenant to do it him/herself.**

4. **Make sure the tenant understands personal responsibility for the day-to-day care of the property.**

   This includes replacing light bulbs and furnace filters, and even fixing clogged toilets that are not caused by plumbing issues.

Rent Receipts

As a landlord, it's your responsibility to issue rent receipts if a tenant requests them. This includes issuing receipts to former tenants who rented from you in the last year. You cannot charge for these receipts.

There are a few key pieces of information that you should include on the receipt:

- Address of the rental property
- Name of tenants on the lease
- Amount and date of all payments received
- Name and signature of the landlord

Not providing a rent receipt when requested to do so, can get you in trouble with the Landlord Tenant Board. Therefore, follow these policies:

1. **Rent receipts are issued at the end of each year for each property, whether the tenant requests it or not.**

2. **In addition to the rent receipt, include a summary of the interest on the last month's rent and the cheque with that interest, if applicable.**

This shows a superior level of organization and ethical conduct on your part. Too many landlords just hope the tenant doesn't know about their right to interest on the last month's rent. Regardless of whether a tenant knows the rule or not, it's our job as landlords to track and pay interest on the last month's rent.

Use this letter to communicate the issuance of last month's rent interest with the tenant:

Date: December 31st, 20XX

Mr. Thomas Tenant, 222 Maple Street

Whitby, Ontario, B2B 2B2

Dear Mr. Tenant:

Please note that included is a cheque for interest on your last month's rent. The interest rate is set by the Ontario government at 2.1% for 20XX and is based on the number of months that you have been renting the property. The amount of the cheque is: $26.25.

Sincerely,

Name of Landlord

Rent Increases

Rents in Ontario are governed by rent control. This means that the Ontario government decides how much that a landlord can increase their rents in a given year. This percentage is based on the consumer price index, but there was a recent change in legislation which set the maximum increase to 2.5% in any given year. Each year, the government posts the increase amount on the Ontario Landlord and Tenant Board web site (http://www.ltb.gov.on.ca). Here is a list of the rental increase over the past 20 years:

Year	Guideline Increase	Year	Guideline Increase
2014	0.8%	2003	2.9%
2013	2.5%	2002	3.9%
2012	3.1%	2001	2.9%
2011	0.7%	2000	2.6%
2010	2.1%	1999	3.0%
2009	1.8%	1998	3.0%
2008	1.4%	1997	2.8%
2007	2.6%	1996	2.8%
2006	2.1%	1995	2.9%
2005	1.5%	1994	3.2%
2004	2.9%		

The tenant must be given the correct written notice of the rental increase at least 90 days before the rent increase takes effect. With few exceptions, the rent for a unit can only be increased if at least 12 months have passed since the tenant first moved in or since the last rent increase.

There are some interesting exemptions to the Ontario rent control rule that many real landlords are unaware of:

1. When a tenant moves out and a new tenant moves in, you can change the rent to whatever amount you would like.

2. If no part of the building was occupied for residential purposes before November 1, 1991, then the rules regarding rental increases in Ontario don't apply. In fact, a landlord can raise the rent as much as they want. In truth, this rarely happens as landlords' rents are usually quite competitive and raising the rent too much could lead to more vacancies.

3. Landlords can also apply directly to the Landlord and Tenant Board for an increase above the rental increase guideline. This usually relates to increased costs due to taxes, utilities, or large scale renovations.

When increasing rent, the goal is to improve cash flow. If the rent raise causes the tenant to leave, the overall cash flow for the year may not improve at all. Follow these policies to carry out rent increases correctly:

1. **Try to keep the rental increase for an existing tenant below $15 per month.**

   A rental increase of $15 or more usually causes tenants to move out. It's usually less expensive to have a tenant stay longer than it is to raise the rent by a few dollars. Vacancies can run two or three months, which amounts to a big loss of income. Having a reliable tenant stay two or three years longer is usually better than risking a re-rental over a few dollars.

2. **If current rent is more than $25 below market, increase rent to avoid being too far behind.**

The above rule about losing a tenant over too much of a rent raise doesn't apply if the rent is too far below market value.

Also, if a property needs to be liquidated, it is easier to sell to an investor if the rent is closer to market value.

3. **If a rent increase is necessary, complete N1 form and include a cover letter explaining the reason for the rent increase.**

This letter should be based on facts. For example, you can state that condo fees or taxes have increased since the beginning of the lease. Sample letter is below

---

Date: June 28th, 20XX
Mr. Thomas Tenant, 222 Maple Street,
Whitby, Ontario, B2B 2B2

Dear Mr. Tenant:

As you are aware, costs of living are constantly going up in today's society.

For your home, the condo fees have increased $120, taxes have increased $100, and insurance has increased $50. If only I could find a way to avoid these three items, I wouldn't need to be giving you this notice. I must do something to cover the increasing cost of home ownership and still be able to maintain the property to a good state of repair.

Therefore, I will need to increase your rent by $25 to $1,275 per month.

This rent increase is equal to 2% which is less than the guideline of 2.1% for 20XX.

As I am required to give you 90 days prior notice, this increase will take effect as of October 1st, 20XX. Therefore, October's rent payment will be $1,275.

Further details can be found in the following legal notice, which, under law, must accompany this letter. If you have any questions please call me at 555-555-5555, or email me at nameoflandlord@email.com, or you may reach me at:

Name of Landlord

111 Oak Street, Whitby,, Ontario, A1A 1A1,

Sincerely,

Name of Landlord

Tenant Insurance

It's highly important that not only you be covered by insurance, but that tenants also be covered. Here are the policies to implement regarding tenant insurance:

1. **You can transfer liability to tenant's insurance.**

   This doesn't mean that you release the $2M commercial liability. Always maintain your own liability insurance, but your insurance company will look to transfer liability to the tenant's insurance. You may require tenants to get tenant insurance in your lease, and you'll be responsible to check that they do if your policy is seeking to transfer liability to a tenant's insurance.

2. **You can make sure that tenants have liability insurance as a rule within the lease.**

3. **Check that tenant has updated insurance and liability coverage annually.**

Request Updated Tenant Information

Follow these policies:

1. Request updated information yearly.

   Never be without current tenant information. If anything has changed pertinent to your tenant, you want to be up to date.

2. Choose one time per year to send out letters to each tenant living in a property longer than 1 year; send all your letters at once.

3. Use a letter similar to the following:

Date: June 28th, 20XX

Mr. Thomas Tenant, 222 Maple Street,
Whitby, Ontario, B2B 2B2

Dear Mr. Tenant:

I hope you're doing well. It's a wonderful time of year to be in Ontario.

You're receiving this letter because you've been with us for over one year! I'd like to take the time to thank you for choosing to live in our property. We rely on excellent tenants, and you've been one of them. Thank you!

One of our yearly tasks is to ensure that we have up to date information for each tenant. This letter is to request that you update any personal information that may have changed since our original records were created.

Please send us the following:
1. Emergency contact number
2. New job position
3. New email
4. New phone number

You may send this information to landlord@email.com or:

Name of Landlord
111 Oak Street,
Whitby,
Ontario, A1A 1A1
Thank you for helping us to do our job well.

Sincerely,

Name of Landlord

Utilities

These policies will streamline your dealings with the utilities:

1. **If you're paying utilities, keep track of the monthly costs in a spreadsheet so it's easy to identify any issues that arise.**

   This can be a good way to identify issues or potential problems. For example, you may notice a spike in the water costs in a particular month. You might have just identified a leak at the property by keeping track of the water bill.

2. **Send a carefully drafted N5 notice if utilities haven't been converted to the tenant's name or if the tenant has inappropriately changed the utilities.**

   Make reference to the lease wording. This will give the tenant 7 days to correct the situation.

   IMPORTANT: To do this, it must state something to this effect in the lease: "The tenant will contract with utility companies and continue that contract for so long as they occupy the unit."

3. **File an L2 application to evict if the tenant fails to correct the situation.**

   If a tenant has agreed to do this and then avoids taking responsibility, it's a bad sign. This means the tenant is trying to avoid paying the bill and is being deceitful. I would find this reason enough to evict.

4. **If there is nothing within the lease regarding utilities, write a letter to the tenant explaining the situation using the specific lease as an example.**

5. **Never transfer any utilities into your personal name or the name of the company.**

   Let the utilities get turned off rather than putting them into your own name. There are only a few exceptions where it could harm the property. For example, having the electricity/gas turned off in the winter and the pipes inside the house freeze.

6. **If, for any reason, the utilities were transferred into your name or the name of the company, gather together all of the current utility bills and start the paperwork for Small Claims Court action.**

Use a transaction ledger to keep track of the bills. As with late rent payment, this allows the judge to easily track your claim. See sample transaction ledger below.

Month	Transaction	Paid	Owed
January	Rent		- $1500
January	Heating Bill		- $90
January	Electricity Bill		- $170
January	Rent	$1500	
Sub-Total		$1500	- 1760
Total			- $260

Cable and Satellite Installs

When tenants desire to have cable or satellite in their property, the provider most often will refuse to install unless they've received written permission from the owner or landlord of the property:

1. You can provide this letter because it would be unfair to deprive tenants of such a common convenience.

2. Use a letter similar to the following:

Date: June 28th, 20XX

Cable Provider Corp,

111 Big Corp. Avenue at, A1A 1A2

Dear Cable Provider Corp:

Name of Landlord grants Cable Provider Corp permission to install cable and satellite in the property tenanted by Mr. Thomas Tenant at: 222 Maple Street, Whitby, Ontario, B2B 2B2

If you have any questions or concerns, please don't hesitate to contact me ---landlordname@email.com or:

Name of Landlord

111 Oak Street,

Whitby,

Ontario, A1A 1A1

Sincerely,

Name of Landlord

Illegal Drugs

The following polices govern illegal drugs:

1. Maintain zero tolerance for illegal drugs.

2. Send an N6 notice immediately if there's a complaint about illegal drug usage.

3. Send a letter and email immediately informing the tenant of the consequences. Use the following letter:

Date: June 28th, 20XX

Mr. Thomas Tenant, 222 Maple Street

Whitby, Ontario, B2B 2B2

Dear Mr. Tenant:

As you know, we have a zero tolerance policy for any illegal activities in the property.

We've received a complaint about illegal drug use in the property. If we receive another complaint, we will be immediately contacting the police.

To comply with the N5 notice you've received, you must cease any illegal drug use or possession immediately.

As stated in the lease, you will be liable for any damage caused by illegal activity in the property.

Sincerely,

Name of Landlord

Unauthorized Pets

The current landlord/tenant laws in Ontario make it almost impossible to evict a tenant based on pets they bring into the rental property after the lease has been signed. However, when a tenant does this, it creates trust issues between the landlord and the tenant. In spite of having your hands tied, I strongly urge you use the following policies:

1. **Ask the tenant to sign an amendment that addresses liability issues related to the pet.**

   This makes the pet owner (rather than the property owner) responsible for any issues caused by the pet. You can't legally force a tenant to sign this, but you can impress upon them that by putting a pet in the property after signing of the lease they were deceptive and that they should take responsibility.

2. **Use an N5 or N7 to evict the tenant if the pet is dangerous or if your specific allergy to the pet would cause a problem with your ability to visit the property (depending on the severity of the problem).**

   As with all Landlord Tenant Board matters you must be able to document the risks a pet poses with times, dates, and locations of specific incidents.

Resident Leaves for Extended Vacation

If a tenant leaves for an extended vacation, it's vital to follow the correct procedure. Remember, you may not be insured if the property is vacant. Use these policies:

1. Inform tenants that they'll need to apprise the landlord when they are leaving on vacation for a week or longer.

2. Instruct tenants to turn off water to the house before leaving on vacation and keep furnace on during winter months.

3. Remind tenants that their insurance will not cover any damages due to water from burst pipes, etcetera when the property is vacant.

4. Inform tenants that they must arrange for a relative or friend to come visit the property every week to ensure the property is in good working order.

5. Provide the person inspecting the property with the landlord's contact number in case of emergencies.

6. Include the tenant extended vacation guidelines in the tenant binder left in the suite.

Landlord Leaves for Vacation

Just as when a tenant leaves, there are special considerations to consider when the landlord leaves for an extended vacation. Follow these policies to ensure success:

1. **Set up phone system.**

   a. Give all tenants the same toll free number to call. If you have access to a telephone during your vacation, change the message to instruct tenants to leave a detailed message and let them know you'll return the call within 24 hours.

   Take your address book on vacation (phone numbers for plumbers, electricians, handyman, and etcetera) and check for messages daily.

   If you don't have easy access to a phone or don't want to deal with it on vacation, pay a family member, friend, real estate agent, or tradesperson to check the messages daily and organize any required repairs.

   b. Specify on cell phone message that you will be away and that the tenant should send an email (check email every couple of days when on vacation).

2. Set up email auto-responder.

The message should explain you're away and provide a number that tenants can call for assistance or emergencies. The number provided in the email auto-responder will go to you or the person you've designated to manage your properties.

3. Pay a real estate professional or contractor, or have a reciprocal agreement with a family member, to manage your properties while you're away.

You may choose to still take and answer calls, or you may have all calls directed to the interim manager. If they have to handle all calls, their workload will be much greater.

If you're taking the calls and only dispatching the interim manager for specific situations, their workload will be less.

4. Have a go-to contractor ready to go.

In some cases, you won't even have to dispatch the interim manager. Instead, you'll send the contractor directly to the property.

5. Give the tenant the go-to contractor's cell phone number.

You may want to instruct a responsible tenant to call the contractor directly. As long as you trust the contractor's discretion, this can be an excellent strategy.

6. Inform both the tenant and the go-to contractor that only emergency repairs will be dealt with while you're away.

Regular maintenance requests are not to be done without your full awareness and approval. Your go-to contractor will be able to discern if the work requested is an emergency or not.

7. **Take care of all the regular maintenance before you go away.**

   This ensures that tenants don't feel like their requests are unimportant. It also shows your proactivity and might even prevent the need for an emergency repair while you're away.

8. **Hire a professional property management service if your portfolio is too large for a family member or other professional, or if you can't find a suitable interim manager.**

   If you go this route, be sure your tenants have been well informed in advance about contact information.

9. **Hand over a spreadsheet with relevant information to the interim manager.**

   This should include descriptions of each property, tenant contact info, condo corporation contact info, insurance info, preferred vendor contact info, copies of each lease, and keys to each property.

   It should also have the name of two or three other people in your investment network to contact for advice if needed.

There are three forms that landlords use depending on the seriousness of the incidents occurring, the **N5**, **N6**, and **N7**.

An **N5** is a Notice to Terminate the Tenancy Early because the tenants, their guest, or an occupant (i.e. child) is damaging the property, interfering with the reasonable enjoyment of the property, interfering with another lawful right or interest of the landlord or another tenant, or there are too many people living in the rental property.

An **N6** is a Notice to Terminate the Tenancy Early because the tenants or another occupant of the rental unit has committed an illegal act.

An **N7** is a Notice to Terminate the Tenancy Early because the tenants, their guest, or another occupant of the rental unit has seriously impaired the safety of another person, wilfully damaged the rental property, used the rental property in a manner that is inconsistent with its use as residential premises, and this has caused or may cause serious damage.

Each of these notices requires that dates and details of the allegations are included in the notice. If you do not file these notices in a manner that is consistent with the requirements of the Landlord Tenant Board, then it is possible that your notices will become void. If you are unsure in any way about completing and serving these notices, you should contact a paralegal or lawyer that specializes in Landlord and Tenant Board matters.

Resident or Pet Damaging Property

This is an important situation to handle correctly. Use the following polices:

1. **Send a letter indicating what damages were caused by the resident or pet.**

   Remind the tenants that the original versus the current condition of the property will be based on the pictures taken at the beginning of tenancy. The pictures were signed by both parties to agree on the move-in condition of the property.

   Remind tenants that they're responsible for repairs and set a time frame for them to be done.

2. **Prepare documentation that shows the previous condition of the property and the current condition of the property.**

3. **Complete N5 form for "willful or negligent damage" or N7 Form for "willful damage."**

   a. Never post an N5/N7 on tenant's door.

   b. Keep a copy of Certificate of Service.

   c. If the N5/N7 is hand delivered, it should have a witness if the tenant is belligerent or ignores communication.

   d. If the N5/N7 is placed in the tenant's mailbox or in between screen door and door, take a picture of the N5/N7 in the mailbox or location it was placed. This should be printed along with the other communication.

Tenant Changes the Lock without Providing Key

This isn't a common problem. In my experience, tenants will usually let you know ahead of time and provide a key. However, if you experience this problem, follow these policies:

1. Let the tenant know immediately that you'll change the lock and charge them if they don't immediately provide you with a key.

   Not only will they have to pay for the change of locks, they'll also have to pay for L8 application fees.

2. File an L8.

   This is an application to the Landlord Tenant Board that gives you legal clout. It tells the tenant directly that they must either provide you with a key or pay for changing the locking system.

3. If they don't immediately comply, change the locks and provide them a key.

4. If the tenant doesn't pay, take them to the Landlord Tenant Board and follow the L8 process to force the tenant to pay you back.

"Success is often achieved by those who don't know that failure is inevitable."

— Coco Chanel

Chapter 11

EMERGENCIES AND EXTENDED VACANCIES

Emergency and Disasters

There are many different emergencies that can occur that are not directly related to the repair of a property. As a landlord, it's vital that you are prepared for emergencies *before* they happen. By the time the emergency happens, it's too late to begin planning. In fact, it's difficult to think clearly when an emergency happens. This is why it's so important to have emergency plans in place. It's far easier to follow a prearranged plan than to invent a new plan on the spot.

Emergencies could include a fire—at the rental or your own home, burglary, flooding, heating loss in winter, long-term power outages, a gas leak, or a severe storm. By preparing for these events, you can hopefully minimize anxiety and property damage.

Ask yourself these questions to better prepare for emergency and disaster:

- Do your tenants have a 24-hour/365 days a year emergency phone number that they can call in case of a disaster or emergency?

- Do you have a communication plan in the event of an emergency?

- Do you have a plan that indicates who a tenant should contact first, second, and third depending on common emergencies?

- Do you have a list of all the emergency contact numbers that the tenant can easily find(e.g. fire, police, ambulance, and utility companies)?

- Do you have evacuation procedures for tenants? Have you clearly communicated them to tenants?

- Are tenants aware that they need tenant insurance and that their possessions would not be covered in a disaster without their own tenant insurance?

- Do tenants have a list of web sites where they can get more information for preparing for a disaster and/or a handbook that they can use in the event of a disaster?

Data Disaster Plan

As discussed elsewhere, data is highly important to a landlord's ability to maintain his/her business. In addition to emergencies in rental properties, a prepared landlord has to consider the possibility of losing physical documents at their own home/office due to a disaster. For this reason, it's imperative that every document is kept in electronic format. Use the following questions to help prepare for a data disruption due to disaster:

- Can you sit at a computer outside of your home/office and carry out normal business procedures without the need to go back to your home/office?

- Do you have a stored list of all banks and account numbers, mortgage numbers, insurance numbers, and other liabilities off site?

- Do you have a stored list of all computer backup data, passwords, and logins for all web sites off site? Are these backups maintained weekly?

- Have you digitally scanned and stored all important documents off site?

Computer Data – Emergency Preparedness

Location/URL	Username	Password	Notes
Google Drive http://drive.google.com	Fake Username	Fake Password	Offsite storage of computer backup
CompanyWebsite.com	Fake Username	Fake Password	Use this to update company website.

Recognizing an Emergency

Follow these policies for recognizing and responding to emergencies:

1. **Understand the types of emergencies that occur in your area. The following are some common disasters:**

   a. Fire

   b. Flooding

   c. Severe Weather

   d. Extreme Heat/Cold

2. **Research how to prepare for these types of disasters. Utilize these emergency preparedness websites:**

   This will inform your practice and help with you to prepare your tenants for an emergency.

   http://www.getprepared.gc.ca/index-eng.aspx

   http://www.ibc.ca/en/Need_More_Info/Home_Insurance_Publications.asp

   http://www.redcross.ca/prepare

   http://www.emergencymanagementontario.ca

3. **Remind tenants to have a disaster plan in place and create a basic emergency kit.**

   This kit should include water for 3 days, food for 3 days with a manual can opener, cans of food, a flashlight with extra batteries, a battery powered or wind-up radio, a first aid kit, cash in small bills and change, and a copy of the tenant emergency plan.

Evaluating an Emergency and Planning a Response

Follow these policies for responding to an emergency:

1. **Remain calm and professional.**

   The quicker you can evaluate the urgency of the disaster, the faster you can ask for help from emergency services. Tenants will be looking to you for leadership in circumstances like these.

2. **Personal safety is always a priority.**

   Don't take unnecessary risks. If you're hurt, you won't be able to help anyone.

3. **Keep tenants informed about the process and the steps you'll be taking in order to address the emergency.**

   This could be in an email to tenants or a voicemail recording.

4. **Remind tenants to pay attention to local news and instructions.**

5. **Remind tenants to complete the "In the Event of a Disaster" form and fax/email/drop it off.**

   This form is designed to get information vital to you in the event of a severe emergency. See sample below:

In the Event of a Disaster

This form should be included in your tenant binder.

Tenant Name: _____

Address of Property: _____

_____

_____

_____

Address/Phone Number where you are vacating: _____

_____

_____

_____

_____

If you are leaving during this disaster, how can we contact you?

_____

_____

_____

Please ensure you can answer yes to the following:

Have You:

- Turned off main water to house?

- Turned off gas line to house?

- Shut-off main electrical breaker to house?

- Secured all items outside of the house?

- Secure property against damage as directed by the local media bulletins?

- Provided contact information?

As a resident of the property, you are responsible for the securing of property.

Please fax or email this to: 555-555-5555 or nameoflandlord@email. com or drop it off at 111 Oak Street, Whitby, Ontario, A1A 1A1

List of Agencies That Assist Tenants

Sometimes, an unfortunate incident will occur. This could be a job loss or the death of a loved one. First and foremost, you're running a business, so rent is due regardless of any difficulty. This doesn't mean that unfortunate events won't take place. In these circumstances, it's a great idea to help tenants find the help they need to get back on their feet. Follow this policy:

1. **Keep a list of agencies and organizations in the area that can provide short-term financial assistance and housing for tenants.**

   If the need arises, you can pass this information along to your tenants. Here are some examples of services in my home region of Durham:

a. **Durham Rent Bank – Community Development Council Durham** – 4-458 Fairall St, Ajax. Ontario L1S 2H5 – 905-686-2661 Fax (905) 686-0984 Toll free 1-866-746-3696

b. **Durham Housing Help** – 4-458 Fairall St, Ajax. Ontario L1S 2H5 – 905-686-2661 Fax 905-686-0984

c. **Durham Emergency Energy Fund** – An interest-free loan program to help qualified Durham residents with energy-related emergencies. Call community development Council Durham at 905-686-2661

d. **The Community Trust Fund** - An interest-free loan program to help qualified Durham residents with emergency housing-related expenses. Call community development Council Durham at 905-686-2661.

Most jurisdictions will have an equivalent version of the services listed here.

"In business, I've discovered that my purpose is to do my best to my utmost ability every day. That's my standard. I learned early in my life that I had high standards."

— Donald Trump

Chapter 12

INFESTATIONS AND COMPLAINTS

Bed Bugs

There are some steps you can take to prevent and remediate bed bugs. Follow these policies:

1. **When screening tenants, review an online bed bug registry like http://bedbugregistry.com/ for a potential tenant's previous addresses.**

   If you do find that the tenant has lived in a bed bug-infested property, this can never be stated as the reason for excluding a tenant from renting a property.

2. **Install bed bug monitoring devices in order to identify whether bed bugs currently exist in a property.**

This puts the tenant at ease knowing that you are on the lookout for bed bugs. If bed bugs are found, immediately begin the process for treatment. Use http://www.epestsolutions.com/bed-bug-traps.html and the *Catchmaster 96* station as your first preference.

3. **Use only a professional exterminator for bed bug remediation.**

Bed bugs are serious business. You can't remove them with homegrown methods. There are freezing, steaming, and chemical treatments, but heat treatments seem to work best. Some people use a combination of both steam *and* chemical treatments. Most treatments include two or more visits. Expect costs of $1200-2400.

4. **Take legal action through small claims court or the Landlord Tenant board if the tenant doesn't fully cooperate with the bed bug treatment.**

Defining who is at fault for the bed bugs may become difficult, but your tenant must at a minimum cooperate fully with remediation. Not cooperating is a valid reason to take legal action.

5. **Have a game plan and discuss the exit strategy with the pest control company.**

There are two ways to detect bed bugs – sight and scent. Doing it by scent involves dogs, so be sure to question your tenants about dog allergies before contracting a company to use this method.

6. **Keep all reports from the company.**

7. **Keep a log of all communication regarding bed bugs and what was done to remedy the situation.**

8. **Always give 24-hour's written notice for entry to a tenant based on the extermination company's timeline.**

Include a document in an email and a letter that lays out what tenants are required to do. The document must inform tenants of their duty to completely cooperate with bed bud remediation efforts and the fact that landlords have the right to evict if tenants don't comply. It must also outline the following steps for preparation:

a. Remove all blankets, sheets, covers, pillows, bath towels and bag them in dissolvable bags for laundering.

b. Wash clothes and linens on hottest recommended settings.

c. Transport in sealed dissolvable bags to prevent movement of insects.

d. Store cleaned and thoroughly dried items in sealed bags labeled 'clean' until chemical treatment is completed.

e. Gather all bedding and wash it in hot water and dry in a hot dryer on highest recommended settings.

f. If you are planning on taking laundry to a laundromat, be sure to have another means to carry your clothes back home.

g. Maintain the highest temperature setting for a minimum of 30 minutes when drying. Items should be hot to the touch upon removal from the dryer. Hot water laundering of items is desirable in conjunction with effective drying but is not absolutely necessary as the dryer temperature will kill the insect stages independently if completed correctly. *Heat treatment of dried items at the highest dryer heat setting is critical in order to kill all life stages of the insect.*

h. Treated items such as shoes, pillows, and plush toys in the dryer on a dryer rack. Manufacturers' recommendations should be followed with alternative treatment methods used if this is contrary to manufacturers' guidelines.

i. Vacuum thoroughly, especially along floor and carpet edges. Use a brush attachment to dislodge eggs and insects.

j. Vacuum along the seams of the mattress and box spring, and tear the back of the box spring off and vacuum there.

k. Vacuum inside drawers and closets, furniture, and everywhere.

l. Sprinkle diatomaceous earth, baking powder, or talc powder; vacuum it up; and remove bag from the property.

m. Dispose of vacuum bags in a sealed plastic bag and remove from the premises immediately.

n. Isolate, wash, and/or steam all vacuum cleaner attachments after final use.

o. Remove and inspect all belongings from furniture, tables, wardrobes, and closets. This includes plastic toys, books and electronics. If free of bed bugs, store in tight fitting containers or bags.

p. Avoid cardboard boxes for storage as insects can hide in the folds and deposit eggs in harbourage areas.

q. All clothing in closets and drawers must be washed as outlined in the above steps. Any clothing that requires dry cleaning will have to be sent to the cleaners.

r. Keep the drawers and closets empty.

s. Removed all items from under the bed, in the closets, and in drawers.

t. Take out all dresser drawers and take apart all beds to expose the framework for the treatment.

u. Move furniture a minimum of 18 inches away from edges.

v. Dismantle bed and other furniture if possible.

w. Hard furniture, floors, and walls should be washed with warm soapy water.

x. Remove pictures, electrical outlets covers, and switch plates from walls.

Take down curtains or drapes and wash or dry clean these, as well; keep them down for the treatment.

y. Eliminate clutter and dispose of items in tightly sealed disposal bags.

z. Ideally, the rooms should be empty of all cloth and plush items except for plush furniture.

aa. Unplug all electrical equipment (televisions, computers, shredders, and etcetera).

bb. Unplugged fish tank filters and cover the top of the tank with plastic during treatment.

cc. Isolate items that cannot be washed or steamed.

dd. Removed and isolate items such as wax candles, lipstick, plants, medicines, food products, wine products, vinyl items, plastic/vinyl blinds, fire extinguishers, and pressurized cans.

ee. Wall hangings, including oil paintings/photographs, may be left in the room.

ff. Remove smoke detectors and batteries throughout the property.

gg. Disengage the sprinkler system.

hh. Protect life safety systems.

ii. Increase house temperature as high as possible.

Bed Bug Detection Dog Inspection Preparation Requirements

As landlord, in addition to preparing tenants for the remediation treatment, you must inform tenants of preparation for the bed bug detection dog. Send a letter with an official notice to enter that includes the following points:

1. All rooms within the inspection area must be open and accessible to the canine detection team.

2. Obstructions throughout the room must be eliminated, especially around the perimeter, beds, and furniture. Bags of clothing must be opened and container lids removed so that the dog may sniff. The Senior Technician will ensure adequate access during a pre-inspection walk through.

3. Residents' pets must be isolated prior to and during the canine detection team's inspection.

4. Ideally, pets will be removed from the premises. If this isn't possible, placement in areas not requiring inspection (such as a bathroom) is acceptable.

5. All food should be placed in containers within cabinets or the refrigerator.

6. Toys, pet food, scratching posts, pet bedding, and water must be removed and non-accessible to the detection dog in all areas to be inspected.

7. Potpourri, deodorizers, and air fresheners must be removed two hours prior to the inspection.

8. All doors and windows should be closed two hours prior to the inspection to minimize draft.

9. Clutter in each room scheduled for inspection must be removed.

10. All bed linens and furniture covers should be removed. Rooms and furniture to be inspected must be swept and vacuumed thoroughly to remove food particles, dusts, spills, and any debris. All trash receptacles in the areas to be inspected must be emptied.

11. Open lockers, file cabinets and storage areas need to be unlocked.

12. Noise and human distraction must be eliminated to ensure the most effective inspection possible. The canine detection team can't work with interference.

13. Air conditioners, heaters, air purifiers, humidifiers, dehumidifiers and ceiling fans must be turned off 30 minutes prior to inspection.

14. All smoking materials must be extinguished and ashtrays removed from the premises two hours prior to inspection.

15. The canine inspection will not take place in environments treated with pesticides or unknown substances within the past 30 days. Landlord should be informed of any pest management efforts and/or treatments— either professional or personally applied—in the 30 days prior to the inspection.

16. Household cleaners or other chemicals should not be used for 12 hours prior to the inspection.

17. The search will be discontinued at the senior technician's discretion if the detection dog's safety is jeopardized.

18. Please inform us of any details that might interfere with scent detection or cause harm to the canine.

19. Additional fees will apply for re-inspections due to inadequate preparation. All preparations must be completed prior to the canine team's arrival.

Pest Control

Follow these policies for pest control:

1. Communicate with tenants about pest control.

   Provide information about pest control policies in the tenant binder.

2. Provide pest control as needed.

3. Inform tenant that he/she must provide access to the property as the landlord deems necessary.

4. If it's determined that the tenant is contributing to the pest problem, the landlord will inform the tenant of changes he/she must make.

5. The tenant may have liability for pest remediation if it's found he/she is culpable for the pest problem.

6. Send this letter if pests are found in the property:

Date: June 28th, 20XX

Mr. Thomas Tenant, 222 Maple Street

Whitby, Ontario, B2B 2B2

Dear Mr. Tenant:

Thank you for informing me of the pests you've found in the property. I appreciate your help in taking care of the problem.

Please include further details about the pests. I require a description of the pest, and dates and locations of where you found the pests. This will help us to focus our investigation into the problem.

It is my job to investigate and remediate the problem. However, if it's found your actions have caused the problem, we may be forced to bill you for remediation. If this is the case, we'll provide specific instructions so that you're aware of how to stop the problem.

Sincerely,

Name of Landlord

Mold in Rental Property

There are two ways to detect mold. One, do a thorough search for it whenever you inspect the property and ask any contractors who are going through the property to watch for mold. Two, educate your tenants about mold and have them notify you if they ever find some. Once mold is found, follow the following polices:

1. Contact the tenants and let them know that you'll be making an appointment to see the problem, and you will have a contractor take care of it.

2. Take pictures of the mold for your records.

3. Contact the appropriate professional to deal with the mold. This could be a regular contractor or a mold remediation company, depending on the scope of the problem.

4. Identify potential causes for the mold and remediate them.

5. If the tenant's actions are making the problem worse, educate them on how to stop mold from forming.

6. Take follow-up pictures after mold is remediated.

7. Let tenant know what's been done to remediate the mold.

8. Once mold is identified in in a property, it is important to take care of it as soon as possible.

9. There are hundreds of types of mold, and not all of them are dangerous, but it takes an expert to decide whether mold is dangerous or not. It's important to take care of mold immediately as it's bad for the house in any case, regardless of whether or not it's dangerous to humans.

10. Once a mold problem is identified, take steps to attack the source of the problem, not just the mold itself.

11. Mold can occur in poorly ventilated areas and in moist areas. Usually it occurs around bathtubs or other parts of bathrooms.

12. Re-caulk or re-paint any area affected by mold once mold is removed.

13. Use a mold-reducing primer such as *Kilz* (or a similar product).

14. Add a bathroom fan if one does not exist or tie in a bathroom fan to the lighting in the bathroom if the issue is poor ventilation in the bathroom.

15. Examine insulation in the attic above the bedroom if the issue is poor bedroom ventilation.

16. Search for any leaks.

17. Clean up a small area—defined as 3 patches or less each under a square meter.

18. Use safety glasses, a disposable dust mask, and household rubber gloves. Scrub washable surfaces with unscented detergent solution and a sponge, then dry it quickly with a clean rag.

19. Clean drywall surfaces with a damp rag using baking soda or a bit of detergent. Do not allow the drywall to get too wet. If mold returns, the source of the moisture hasn't been removed.

20. Clean up a moderate area—defined as one or more patches larger than a square meter but smaller than 3 square meters.

21. Use a disposable dust mask, safety goggles, and household rubber gloves. Isolate affected area by taping plastic sheeting to the walls and ceiling. Use the same cleanup procedure as with small area.

22. Clean up an extensive area—defined as an area larger than a 4 x 8 feet.

23. In extreme cases of mold, consider hiring Kate and Associates, Inc. http://www.molddog.ca, or a similar service. Using a professional mold remediation company guarantees that the problem will not come back.

Noise Complaints – Small Multi-Family

If the noise complaint happens in a small multi-unit property, follow these policies for remedying the situation:

1. **The first time a tenant complains about noise, send an email and letter to both sets of residents letting them know the need to work things out.**

   Sample letter below:

Date: June 28th, 20XX
Mr. Thomas Tenant, Unit 1, 222 Maple Street
Whitby, Ontario, B2B 2B2

Mr. Rick Renter
Unit 2, 222 Maple Street, Whitby, Ontario, B2B 2B2

Dear Mr. Tenant and Mr. Renter:

As you know, both of your residences are in one house. This is something you were aware of when you moved in.

Although we have made efforts to separate and deaden sounds between the units beyond what you'd find in most two-unit properties, it's still only one house. The units are not soundproof. It's expected there will be a reasonable amount of noise from each unit.

Knowing this is a two-unit property, I would appreciate it if you could both continue to make adjustments, both in your sensitivity to normal noise and in your efforts to limit it.

Sincerely,

Name of Landlord

---

2. **If the problem escalates, talk to each set of residents separately.**

Mediate an accommodation regarding the times of the noise. Make sure both sets of tenants are clearly aware of the specific nature of the other tenant's complaints. Ask if they can resolve their specific issue.

3. **You might consider filing an N5 Notice.**

Noise Complaints – Single Family Homes

If the noise complaint pertains to a single-family home, use the following policies:

1. Always take note of names, dates, and times in a written log.

Follow this rule whether the complaint comes from a neighbour or another tenant in the same property.

The first time it occurs, mention the compliant and send an email and letter asking them to take note of the noise.

2. In the letter, mention the possibility of issuing an N5 - Notice to End a Tenancy Early.

3. If there's a second noise complaint, include the names, dates, and times and include a much firmer letter (sample below).

4. The termination date of the N5 must be 20 days after the date the N5 is given (be sure to complete a certificate of service).

The tenant has seven days to correct the problem. In the case of a noise complaint, this means they mustn't be noisy during the next seven days. If the tenant doesn't correct the problem within seven days, the N5 allows for beginning of the eviction process due to a landlord's right to enjoyment of the property.

Date: August 28th, 20XX

Mr. Thomas Tenant, 222 Maple Street

Whitby, Ontario, B2B 2B2

Dear Mr. Tenant:

As you're already aware, the obligations of your lease require that "Tenants will be mindful of excessive noise between the hours of 11:00 pm and 7:00 am."

We have received complaints regarding excessive noise on June 27th at11:25pm as was mentioned in our previous letter and N5 notice and now again on August 27th at 11:45pm. We are issuing a second N5 notice - "Notice to End a Tenancy Early".

The Residential Tenancies Act states the following if notice is not given in accordance with the Act:

Termination for cause, reasonable enjoyment

64. (1) A landlord may give a tenant notice of termination of the tenancy if the conduct of the tenant, another occupant of the rental unit, or a person permitted in the residential complex by the tenant is such that it substantially interferes with the reasonable enjoyment of the residential complex for all usual purposes by the landlord or another tenant or substantially interferes with another lawful right, privilege, or interest of the landlord or another tenant. 2006, c. 17, s. 64 (1).

Please follow the instructions on the N5 document.

Sincerely,

Name of Landlord

5. Issue a second N5 notice if the noise complaints continue within 6 months of the first N5.

6. The second N5 must include a termination date of 14 days after the date when the notice is served. There's no opportunity for the tenant to correct the problem and void the notice.

7. Send a new letter once the second N5 is issued.

See sample letter below:

Date: June 28th, 20XX
Mr. Thomas Tenant, 222 Maple Street
Whitby, Ontario, B2B 2B2

Dear Mr. Tenant:

As you're aware, the obligations of your lease require that "Tenants will be mindful of excessive noise between the hours of 11:00 pm and 7:00 am."

We have received complaints regarding excessive noise on June 27th at 11:25pm. As mentioned in our previous email, we are issuing an N5 - "Notice to End a Tenancy Early".

The Residential Tenancies Act states the following if notice is not given in accordance with the Act:

Termination for cause, reasonable enjoyment:

64. (1) A landlord may give a tenant notice of termination of the tenancy if the conduct of the tenant, another occupant of the rental unit, or a person permitted in the residential complex by the tenant is such that it substantially interferes with the reasonable enjoyment of the residential complex for all usual purposes by the landlord or another tenant or substantially interferes with another lawful right, privilege or interest of the landlord or another tenant. 2006, c. 17, s. 64 (1).

Please follow the instructions on the N5 document.

Sincerely,

Name of Landlord

---

8. Be prepared with documentation and witnesses (those who made the complaint) in order to end the tenancy at the Landlord Tenant Board.

It's vital you have all of your notes, filings, and witnesses prepared. Without any of these, it will be difficult to win at tribunal.

For any Repair or Maintenance Item

Use these policies for any repair or maintenance request:

1. A repair or replacement is justified if the repair or replacement is brought about by normal wear.

   a. A repair to a leaking faucet is justified.

   b. A repair to a new hole in the wall is not and must be paid for by the tenant.

2. Don't repair, replace, or upgrade if something functions within normally accepted parameters.

   If a tenant requests work that you're prohibited from doing based on your policy, be sure to explain this calmly to tenants and deflect any indication that the decision is personal; it's strictly business policy, and you can't bend it.

   You may choose to word your letter, email, or phone conversation like this: "I'd love to replace both the dryer and the shower head, but I've agreed with my bank and my accountant that this repair policy has to be maintained. They insist on it as a condition of this business."

   This removes the perception that you're the mean landlord. It's the banker's and accountant's fault.

Request for Repairs from Tenants

Use these policies for tenant repair requests:

1. **Repairs should be made in writing.**

   There should be 5-10 repair requests included in the Tenant Binder when the property is rented out.

2. **These repairs should be grouped together into three or more repairs.**

   This will keep the cost down and make best use of the contractor's

3. **Setup a weekly or monthly maintenance schedule.**

   Don't rush over to do a repair the minute a tenant requests it. You'll save time and money by scheduling times for maintenance.

4. **Minor repairs should only be done after contractors have completed major repairs.**

   This is because the minor repair may have to be redone after the major repair. Or the major repair may cause damage to the minor repair. An example would be painting a bathroom before a toilet is changed. The walls may get dented while the toilet is being changed and you'd have to repair the walls and paint them again.

If the tenants are responsible for causing the repair or maintenance issue, then they should be paying for it. This commonly occurs with toilets or other plumbing related issues, but could relate it to any number of repairs. You can make the repair—just be sure to charge them for the repair.

Here is a sample letter that you can use:

Date: August 28th, 20XX
Mr. Thomas Tenant, 222 Maple Street
Whitby, Ontario, B2B 2B2

Dear Mr. Tenant:

As you're already aware, on August 14th we had a contractor complete the following repair: **Describe the Repair**

This repair was identified as being caused by improper use of the
_____.

The Residential Tenancies Act states the following:

34. The tenant is responsible for the repair of undue damage to the rental unit or residential complex caused by the wilful or negligent conduct of the tenant, another occupant of the rental unit or a person permitted in the residential complex by the tenant. 2006, c. 17, s. 34.

Please pay the attached bill within 30 days.

Sincerely,

Name of Landlord

Air Conditioner Troubleshooting

Follow these procedures for tenant air conditioner complaints:

1. Check that there's power to the air conditioner unit.

2. If there seems to be no apparent problems with the AC unit itself, check at the control panel that all the wires are connected properly.

3. If all seems okay and the problem persists, call an HVAC technician.

Heater Troubleshooting

Use this set of procedures for tenant heater complaints:

1. Check to ensure that the batteries in the thermostats are working.

2. Check that all air vents are clear of debris.

3. If rooms at one end of the house are pushing out more air than the other end of the house, check that the air dampeners are closed at the opposite end of the house where the problem exists.

   By doing this you are balancing the air in the home.

4. Clean the air vents.

5. If all seems okay and the problem persists, call an HVAC technician.

Fridge Troubleshooting

Follow this fridge complaint procedure:

1. Clean dust or debris from the back of the fridge.

2. Call a technician if cleaning doesn't help.

Dryer Troubleshooting

Follow this procedure for tenant dryer complaints:

1. Check dryer lint trap.

2. Check dryer exhaust for lint and buildup.

3. Check hose and exhaust for buildup or kinks in the hose (always use a metal exhaust hose).

4. Check that the dryer is not being overloaded.

5. Check that the dryer is not drying heavy materials.

6. Try regular cycle for five minutes to see if it gets hot – Open door.

7. Try regular cycle for five minutes to see if it's tumbling – open door.

8. Turn on dryer and go outside to check the air flow from the dryer vent. If vent is blocked, this will affect the electricity consumption, too.

9. Remove exhaust, turn on dryer, and check air flow from dryer.

10. Try using the timer to dry clothes because the problem could be with the automatic cycle.

11. Check to see if dryer is under warranty.

12. Call related dryer company if it's under warranty.

13. Call a technician.

14. Replace the dryer with a used appliance. Preferably with a warrenty.

15. Replace the dryer with a scratch and dent appliance with a company that will service your appliance; then you will not have to deal with it again for a long time.

Showerhead Troubleshooting

Tenants will sometimes complain about the following showerhead problems: water flow too strong, water flow not strong enough, showerhead doesn't have the setting they want. Use the following suggestions to deal with showerhead complaints:

1. Check the showerhead with the tenant. Remove it by twisting where the showerhead meets the hose. Look for worn washers that might be affecting the flow of water.

2. Check whether the showerhead is adjustable. If so, make adjustment.

3. Reduce water flow to the bathroom via the shut off valve—basement area or near the shower—if it has one.

4. Adjust water via the tap so there is less pressure going through the shower head.

5. If it is an un-adjustable shower control, look into changing the showerhead as it's likely using too much water. Use a low flow showerhead. This will mean a lower water bill.

6. Test the showerhead and find out what your tenants mean. If there's nothing wrong and they still complain, take the old one off, have the tenants buy one, and they can take it with them when they move out.

Showing Properties

Use these policies and procedures for showing properties:

1. Bring something to do while you are waiting to show a property or meet a repairman. Make phone calls, do paperwork, or check out the unit for repairs/improvements.

2. If tenants want to leave their lease early, inform them that it will be dependent upon you finding another tenant. Explain that they need to keep the property spotless so it will be easier to sell.

3. When purchasing a property, see if you can get a clause for showing the property before you close on it.

Show the property to several prospective tenants at the same time to create a competitive environment.

4. When selling a property that's currently a rental, you have to have a high level of coordination with the tenant.

Some tenants will only want the listing realtor to show the property. You must always respect tenants' rights and give them proper notice to show the property. Have your realtor arrange multiple showings in a certain window of time.

Note: The purchaser must automatically assume a tenant if the closing date is before the tenant's lease expires. The exception to this rule is if the tenant agrees to move out on a date prior to possession.

IN CONCLUSION

I hope that this book will help you to enjoy the successes that our family has enjoyed managing our rental properties. If you can avoid some of the common mistakes that real estate investors and landlords make while managing rental properties, then this book will have been a great success.

You might be surprised that a tenant will send you a thank you card or a little present for being such a wonderful landlord by mastering the art and science of good relationships. You can use real estate to create prosperity for your family now, by watching your cash flow, as well as create generational wealth by being able to manage and hold your properties for a long time. By following the policies and procedures outlined in this book, you will find that you have guidelines that will help to make property management easier.

Be sure to visit http://www.theontariolandlordtoolbox.com/ in order to download some of the resources mentioned in this book, updates to the book, as well as the publication of future books.

RESOURCES AND APPENDICES

Stay Up To Date on Laws and Get Support

The Ontario Landlord Tenant Act is tilted in the tenant's favour. It's your job as a landlord and property manager to stay on top of new information. There are a few key websites that can provide you with support and information:

1. Landlord Self-Help Centre – http://www.landlordselfhelp. com/ – This a non-profit community legal clinic which supports Ontario's small-scale landlord community exclusively. You can call them during business hours for answers to specific questions.

2. Landlord and Tenant Board – http://www.ltb.gov.on.ca – This is the Ontario Landlord Tenant Board web site. You can call and ask customer service for information about the Residential Tenancies Act, but they will not give legal advice.

3. Residential Tenancies Act – http://www.elaws.gov.on.ca/ html/statutes/english/elaws_statutes_06r17_e.htm – Here you can find the text of the entire Residential Tenancies Act.

4. CanLII – http://canlii.ca/en/on/onltb/index.html – Searchable database of recent decisions from the Landlord Tenant Board. Reviewing these cases can be very helpful.

WEB SITES MENTIONED

- The Ontario Landlord Toolbox – **www.theontariolandlordtoolbox.ca** – This is the web site that supports this book. Find more resources online.

- Carol's Furnished Rentals – **www.carolsfurnishedrentals.com** – Example of a local entrepreneur that specializes in furnished rentals.

- Insurance Bureau of Canada – **www.ibc.ca** – Information on Tenant Contents Insurance and other insurance products.

- Crime and Trauma Cleaning Service – **www.gtaclean.com** and **www.crimescenecleaners.ca**

- Get Prepared - **www.getprepared.gc.ca** – Canadian Emergency Preparedness

- Red Cross – **www.redcross.ca** – Emergency Guidelines and Resources

- Emergency Management Ontario -**www.emergencymanagementontario.ca** – Latest information on emergencies affecting Ontarians

- ePestSolutions – **www.epestsolutions.com/bed-bug-traps.html** – Bed bug traps and monitors

- Mould Dog – **www.molddog.ca** – Indoor mould testing with Certified Mould Detection Dog

- Quickbooks – **quickbooks.intuit.com** – Accounting and bookkeeping software

- Accountant in a Box – **accountantinabox.ca** – Gives you tips and tricks to use the key features of Quickbooks which will be helpful with the bookkeeping side of your business.

- Landlord Self-Help Centre – **www.landlordselfhelp.com** – This a non-profit community legal clinic which supports Ontario's small-scale landlord community exclusively. You can call them during business hours for answers to specific questions.

- Landlord and Tenant Board – **www.ltb.gov.on.ca** – This is the Ontario Landlord Tenant Board web site. You can call customer service for information about the Residential Tenancies Act, but they will not give legal advice.

- Residential Tenancies Act – **www.elaws.gov.on.ca/html/statutes/english/elaws_statutes_06r17_e.htm** – Here you can find the text of the entire Residential Tenancies Act.

- CanLII – **canlii.ca/en/on/onltb/** – Searchable database of recent decisions from the Landlord Tenant Board. Reviewing these cases can be very helpful.

RECOMMENDED BOOKS

Real Estate Riches: A Money-Making Game Plan for the Canadian Investor by Tahani Aburaneh

Spend Smarter, Save Bigger, by Margot Bai

Legal, Tax and Accounting Strategies for the Canadian Real Estate Investor by Steve Cohen and George Dube's

Investing in Rent to Own Property by Mark Loeffler

From Renos to Riches: The Canadian Real Estate Investor's Guide to Practical and Profitable Renovations by Ian Szabo

Fix & Flip: The Canadian How-To Guide for Buying, Renovating, and Selling Property For Fast Profit by Mark Loeffler and Ian Szabo

ABOUT THE AUTHOR

Quentin D'Souza is a highly respected multiple award winning Real Estate Investor in the Ontario Real Estate Investing community. He has appeared in and quoted in, many different real estate publications and books.

He is a trusted authority on the Durham Real Estate Market. Quentin has worked with and mentored thousands of Real Estate Investors through the Durham Real Estate Investor Club over the last 5 years.

Quentin manages a large real estate portfolio, while still having a very full life outside of real estate. You will often find him at one of his two son's sports events or activities.

www.ingramcontent.com/pod-product-compliance
Lightning Source LLC
Chambersburg PA
CBHW060353220326
41598CB00023B/2911